A MODULAR AND EXTENSIBLE NETWORK
STORAGE ARCHITECTURE

Distinguished Dissertations in Computer Science

Edited by
C.J. van Rijsbergen, University of Glasgow

The Conference of Professors of Computer Science (CPCS), in conjunction
with the British Computer Society (BCS), selects annually for publication
up to four of the best British PhD dissertations in computer science. The
scheme began in 1990. Its aim is to make more visible the significant
contribution made by Britain – in particular by students – to computer
science, and to provide a model for future students. Dissertations are selected
on behalf of CPCS by a panel whose members are:

C.B. Jones, Manchester University (Chairman)
S. Abramsky, Imperial College, London
H.G. Barrow, University of Sussex
D.A. Duce, Rutherford Appleton Laboratory
M.E. Dyer, University of Leeds
D. May, Inmos Ltd, Bristol
V.J. Rayward-Smith, University of East Anglia
M.H. Williams, Heriot-Watt University

CAMBRIDGE UNIVERSITY PRESS
Cambridge, New York, Melbourne, Madrid, Cape Town,
Singapore, São Paulo, Delhi, Tokyo, Mexico City

Cambridge University Press
The Edinburgh Building, Cambridge CB2 8RU, UK

Published in the United States of America by Cambridge University Press, New York

www.cambridge.org
Information on this title: www.cambridge.org/9780521349468

First published 1995
First paperback edition 2011

A catalogue record for this publication is available from the British Library

ISBN 978 0 521 55115-1 Hardback
ISBN 978-0-521-34946-8 Paperback

A MODULAR AND EXTENSIBLE NETWORK STORAGE ARCHITECTURE

SAI-LAI LO
Downing College Cambridge
Research Engineer, Olivetti Research Limited, Cambridge

CAMBRIDGE
UNIVERSITY PRESS

To my parents

Contents

List of Figures

List of Tables

Trademarks

UNIX is a registered trademark of AT&T.
NFS is a trademark of Sun Microsystems, Inc.

Glossary

This list defines abbreviations and some technical terms used in the text.

ATM Asynchronous Transfer Mode.

BSC Byte Segment Custode. A physical storage layer custode that implements the byte segment abstraction.

byte segment A physical storage layer object which abstracts the secondary storage device.

CFC Continuous-media File Custode. A logical storage layer custode that implements the continuous-media file abstraction.

CSCAN Circular SCAN. A disk scheduling algorithm.

continuous-media Data types, such as digital video and audio, which are sequences of discrete and temporally related data samples.

continuous-media file A file type to store continuous-media data.

custode n. One who has the custody of anything- Oxford English Dictionary 1971. A server of MSSA.

DCE Distributed Computing Environment. A network of client workstations with shared resources provided by a group of servers.

FFC Flat File Custode. A logical storage layer custode that implements the flat file abstraction.

flat file A synonym of byte-stream file. This corresponds to the file abstraction of conventional filing system such as UNIX.

logical storage layer The upper layer of MSSA and consists of different file custodes. Each custode implements a file abstraction.

LS layer See logical storage layer.

MSSA The Multi-Service Storage Architecture. A network storage service design investigated in this dissertation.

NVRAM Non-volatile random access memory.

physical storage layer The lower layer of MSSA and consists of byte segment custodes.

PS layer See physical storage layer.

SATF Shortest access time first. A disk scheduling algorithm.

SFC Structured File Custode. A LS layer custode that implements the structured file abstraction.

structured file A file type of MSSA which can store arbitrary user-defined structures.

UPS Uninterruptible power supply

Value-adding client A client of MSSA that provides a service to other clients.

Preface to this edition

This edition is largely an un-edited version of my dissertation that was submitted over a year ago. An index is added to help readers to locate the sections of interest to them. The work that is described in this book is part of a research project[1] that I continued to work on for another year after I had written my dissertation. In a way this book represents a snapshot of an ongoing project that continues to evolve, as any active research work should be.

Some of the ideas described here have been further developed and refined. More flexible use of access control lists has been introduced. The identifiers used in the system are no longer structured, hence the name space is more efficiently used and value-adding clients are better supported. Stream interleaving is introduced to allow the continuous-medium custode to deliver streams with a dynamic range of quality of service. Over the past year or so, my colleagues and I at the Computer Laboratory, University of Cambridge, have completed the implementation of most components described in this book.

However I have resisted the temptation to update the text, partly to keep in line with the spirit of this book series, and partly because I believe the design principles, which are the main contributions of my work, have not been changed. I shall leave it to our publications more recently to report the progress of this project.

I wish to thank the selection committee, chaired by Professor van Rijsbergen of the University of Glasgow, for the honour of receiving this distinguished dissertation award and the Cambridge University Press for publishing this work.

---

[1]The project is funded by the UK EPSRC grant GR/H 13666.

Preface

I would like to thank my superviser, Jean Bacon, for her advice, encouragement, and practical assistance during the course of this research.

I am grateful to Ken Moody and members of the System Research Group for their valuable advice and helpful discussions. Tim Wilson, Sue Thomson, Glenford Mapp and Richard Hayton deserve special mention. I am also grateful to the past and present members of the Laboratory who develop and maintain the WANDA system. This target platform is instrumental to the experimental work that was done in this research. I appreciate the assistance provided by Jean Bacon, Ken Moody, Richard Hayton, Glenford Mapp, Robert Sultana, Tim Wilson and John Bates who suggested improvements to the dissertation.

I am deeply grateful to my family for their love and support. My parents' unceasing emphasis on education and assiduousness has provided me with many opportunities.

I am indebted to the finiancial support provided by the Croucher Foundation and the Science and Engineering Research Council.

Except where otherwise stated in the text, this dissertation is the result of my own work and is not the outcome of work done in collaboration.

I hereby declare that this dissertation is not substantially the same as any I have submitted for a degree or diploma or any other qualification at any other university.

I further state that no part of my dissertation has already been, or is being currently submitted for any such degree, diploma or other qualification.

1

Introduction

1.1 What is a network storage service?

A network storage service is a long term data repository in a Distributed Computing Environment (DCE) through which users may collaborate and share information resources.

Typically, users gain access to a DCE through workstations and share resources, such as computation servers, network gateways, etc, on the network. Similarly, the task of providing long term data storage for all the storage needs in a DCE is better met by a network storage service than by scattered and localised workstation storage. There are several reasons. Firstly, for economic reasons, there is often a strong incentive to share resources. Secondly, as the data stored on computers are a vital asset to users and form the primary input and product of information processing, it is of great importance that the security, integrity and availability of the data be maintained and the data be retrieved efficiently. Data security can only be enforced if the data are completely under the control of a trusted authority. Data integrity requires protective measures, such as routine backup, and to be administered to guard against storage media failure and user errors. Data availability demands speedy recovery from system faults or data replication to mask out system failures. The demand for speedy data access can best be met by exploiting the latest advances in hardware and software technologies through purpose built servers. All these criteria favour a network storage service under centralised administration.

Distributed file systems are today's state-of-the-art network storage service. A distributed file system stores files which are named objects that are created and destroyed by the system in response to explicit external commands. The files remain in existence and are immune to temporary system failures until their explicit destruction.

An important characteristic of (distributed) file systems is that they do not know the type and the logical relationships of stored data items. This is the most important difference between a (distributed) file system and a (distributed) database. Data items in the latter can be accessed associatively according to some user specified predicates.

1

1.2   Research Motivation

This work observes that contemporary distributed file systems are optimised to store text and binary data. Structured and continuous-medium data are becoming important data types. Digital audio and video are examples of continuous-medium data now being deployed in computing environments. These data types are very different from conventional text and binary and cannot be supported by distributed file systems.

Furthermore, contemporary distributed file systems are designed in a highly vertical integrated fashion and do not provide a proper framework for extensions. Extensibility is necessary both in enhancing the storage service functionalities and for the utilisation of new storage device types and data placement/migration strategies.

1.3   Research Statement

This work proposes a new network storage service design– the Multi-Service Storage Architecture (MSSA).

MSSA conforms to the file storage model, i.e. objects are stored and retrieved by names. However, MSSA is different from contemporary distributed file systems because it supports multiple file abstractions. Contemporary distributed file systems only support the UNIX-style flat (or byte-stream) file abstraction. MSSA supports others, such as the structured and continuous-medium file abstractions, as well.

MSSA is also structurally different from contemporary distributed file systems. Modularity and Extensibility are the main emphases of this work. Common functionalities are factored into layers. Each layer adds value to the services provided by the set of lower layers. This multi-layer approach to support new data types also distinguishes MSSA from other work on new data type support, especially in the field of continuous-medium data storage.

1.4   Dissertation Outline

Chapter 2 reviews the development of distributed file systems and points to the limitations of these systems. The chapter also discusses several emerging trends which will have significant impact on the design of storage services. The discussion concludes that a new approach to storage service design is necessary.

Chapter 3 summarises the previous observations into four goals that MSSA should achieve. This is followed by a presentation of the MSSA framework. MSSA internally is a two-layer architecture which supports different file abstractions. The chapter also defines the interface between the two layers and introduces the notion of sessions which is a new way to specify performance requirements dynamically.

Chapter 4 and 5 address several issues that must be tackled with common policies in all file abstractions. These include access control, naming, object location, and existence control.

Chapter 6 presents the design of a byte segment custode (BSC) which is a lower layer component of MSSA. The BSC provides atomic update semantics with a transaction mechanism. The transaction mechanism uses non-volatile memory to achieve high perfor mance. Its performance is evaluated in chapter 7.

Chapter 8 discusses the concept and interface of *rate-based* sessions. *Rate-based* sessions allow the upper layer to obtain temporal performance guarantee from the lower layer in order to support the real time delivery of continuous-medium data.

Chapter 9 describes a prototype implementation of *rate-based* sessions and presents an evaluation of its performance.

Chapter 10 concludes this dissertation with a summary of the lessons learned and some suggestions for future work.

2

Background

2.1 Introduction

The purpose of this chapter is to establish the context for discussion in the rest of this dissertation. This work is motivated by the recognition that contemporary distributed file systems have basic assumptions that limit their applicability to newly emerged data types and applications. To understand these limitations, it is important to look at the development of distributed file systems in the past 15 years (section 2.2) and the design tradeoffs that have been made (section 2.3).

The progress in computer technologies has brought about new applications which were not possible only a few years ago. However, these applications also brought about new problems that must be solved. In sections 2.4,2.5,2.6 and 2.7, four emerging trends that have significant impact on the design of network storage services are discussed. This chapter concludes with an assertion that a holistic design restructuring is necessary.

2.2 The Development of Distributed File Systems

The earliest model of file sharing, dating back to the early 70s, involved user-initiated file transfers between two machines on the computer network. Users were fully aware of the distinction between local and remote files, both in naming convention and permitted operations. Today, this approach is no longer regarded as a distributed file system. Nevertheless, file transfer programs such as FTP [Bhu71] and FTAM [fta85] are still used to share files, especially over national or global networks.

The ability to perform the same set of operations on both local and remote files was soon recognised as an important property of distributed file systems. In fact, this property, commonly known as network transparency, has since become a fundamental requirement which affects many aspects of distributed file system design.

In the early 80s, there was considerable interest in providing **atomic transactions** and **concurrency control** in distributed file systems. Transaction support was considered a

5

useful mechanism to prevent inconsistencies arising from machine and communication failures or concurrent access to files by other clients. Felix [FO81], XDFS [SMI80], Alpine [BKT85], Swallow [Svo81] are examples of such systems. Since then, the UNIX-style byte stream file model [Bac86] [MJLF84] [POS90] has been adopted by most distributed file systems. None of these provides direct transaction support. As the systems are mainly used for program development and engineering applications, this is considered a reasonable tradeoff between high performance and the possible danger of having occasional data inconsistency.

The Cambridge File Server (CFS) [Dio80], developed in the early 80s, differed from other designs in the same period in one significant respect. The Cambridge design is a capability-based virtual disc system augmented with a naming substrate which provides the desired coherency without committing the clients to any specific directory structures or textual name conventions. The CFS was used to support two file systems (Tripos [RN83] and the CAP filing system [Del80]), an object-based file store [Cra86] and a digital voice store [Cal87].

Since the mid-80s, researchers have explored the use of **data caching** on diskless or dataless[1] workstations to improve the performance of remote file serving. The cache consistency problem is addressed in different ways depending on the models of data sharing adopted by the different designs. The Cedar File System [SGN85], which was the first caching file system, eliminates the cache consistency problem by forcing all files to be immutable. Sun's Network File System (NFS) [Sun89] does not define clearly what guarantees the system makes about the consistency of the client caches. In most NFS implementations, data are used directly from the cache if it has been validated within some time period, usually a few seconds. Andrew [HKM+88], MFS [Bur88] and Sprite [NWO88], developed around the same time, adopt different write-sharing models and assume a different granularity of sharing. Hence the cache consistency protocols of the three designs are quite different. A comparison of the relative merits of the various cache consistency protocols is contained in [Bur88].

The **availability** of distributed file systems has been a concern of researchers for many years. LOCUS [WPE+83] is an early example which combined replication and an algorithm to detect inconsistency to achieve high availability. In the past few years, there has been considerable interest in using file replication to achieve high availability. Echo [HBM+89], Coda [SKK+90], Harp [LGG+91] and Deceit [SBM89] are examples of highly available distributed file systems. The systems differ from earlier designs in that they are all Unix-style file systems and have combined client caching with server replication.

Disconnected operation forms a new strand of work in distributed file system research. This line of work recognises the importance of mobile computing and the need to support automatic data consolidation when a portable computer is reconnected to a distributed computing environment (DCE). Coda [KS91] is the first system to support this mode of computing.

Distributed file system has been an active area of research for nearly two decades. It is not possible to cover, in this limited discussion, all the significant work. More detailed accounts can be found in [Svo84] [LS90]. However, it is clear from the discussion above

---

[1]This refers to workstations which have local disks set up as virtual memory paging store and/or temporary file systems only.

that distributed file systems have been designed to fulfill four requirements: efficiency, transparency, reliability and security.

In other words, a distributed file system should be as *efficient* to use as local file systems and yet its distributed nature should be *transparent* to users. As a shared resource, its capacity and performance have to be *scalable* to match the increase in the size of the system. Being a central point for data sharing, it has to be *reliable* and highly *available*. Finally, it has to be adequately *secure* to prevent unauthorised access to valuable data stored in the system.

However, like other engineering work, the design of distributed file systems always involves tradeoffs between desirable system behaviour and the cost and limitation of hardware and software technologies.

2.3   Limitations of Today's Distributed File Systems

In distributed file system research, many well tried ideas are highly dependent on the *physical* and *usage* characteristics of data. The size distribution of files, the access pattern, the update pattern, the degree of concurrent access, the granularity of concurrent access, the availability requirement and the level of tolerance towards loss of data in events of system failures, etc., are all important design considerations.

For example, client caching plays a very important role in the success of distributed file systems. The implicit assumption is that the client access pattern exhibits good locality of reference and client caches are large enough to achieve a high hit rate. Also, the cache consistency protocols assume low levels of concurrent write-sharing. For instance, the early version of AFS [HKM+88] only supports whole file caching and sequential write sharing because these were thought to be the common characteristics of data sharing in a DCE. Although the derivative of AFS— OSF DEcorum [KLA+91]— and other caching file systems [Bur88] [NWO88] support strict single-system semantics, these systems are likely to operate efficiently only if the degree of concurrent sharing is low.

Some research work on improving the performance of file systems relies heavily on the observed access patterns to make the design tradeoffs. The Bullet file server [vRTW89] is one example. The designers observed that most files in the file system they had studied were small in size and were usually accessed in their entirety. To take advantage of larger main memory and higher capacity disks and to optimise for performance, the bullet file server only supports immutable files which are stored contiguously on disk. Files are cached in their entirety in RAM on the server. When compared with the SUN NFS using simple tests [vRST88], the designers claim that their server performs favourably and is 3 to 6 times faster on reads. However the design has a major potential drawback in that its functionality and performance would be degraded far more severely than more conventional file system designs, such as the Unix FFS [MJLF84], when the data properties are not what the designers expect. For instance, the strict immutability of files requires new copies be created for every update and the extra overhead of copying old data would become intolerable for frequent, and perhaps small step, updates.

Similarly, log-structured file systems, such as Sprite LFS [RO91], are designed with the assumption that large client caches will have the effect of shifting the server work load towards being write-dominated. The basic principle of this work is to collect large amounts of new data in a file cache in main memory and then write the data to disk in a single large disk write that can use all of the disk's bandwidth. However, this idea is complicated by the need to maintain large free areas on disk. Rosenblum reports that a simple cleaning policy based on cost and benefit analysis works well with some simulated and real work loads.

The issue of interest in this dissertation is not whether these techniques are suitable for today's research and engineering environments where the main data types are text and binaries and the principal activities are software development, engineering simulations and text processing. Rather, the assertion here is that new data types, which will be discussed in section 2.4, are very different from conventional data types in terms of *physical* and *usage* characteristics. Therefore, contemporary distributed file systems, being limited by their basic design assumptions, are unable to support the new data types.

Also, file servers are designed in a highly vertical integrated fashion and there is little room for extension. It would be difficult to extend such a design to accommodate new data types or other functional enhancements. Apart from the need to support new data types, there are other incentives to move towards a more extensible design. The incentives identified in this dissertation are: better support for structured data (section 2.5), extensions to primary storage functions (section 2.6) and better data placement strategies (section 2.7).

2.4 Support of Continuous-Medium Data

Digital video and audio are the latest members of information media being used in a computing environment. They are called continuous-media because, unlike other information types, there is an inherent temporal relationship between the sequence of discrete data samples of which they are composed.

A continuous-medium sequence is transmitted from one end point to another in real-time as a stream of data samples. The sequence has an inherent temporal function which determines when each data sample should be presented at the receiving end. Unfortunately, the data path between the two end points can introduce delay and delay variations (referred to as jitter). Therefore, it is necessary to control the magnitude of jitter to ensure an acceptable quality of presentation. Moreover, a multi-media presentation can, by definition, consist of more than one continuous-medium sequence. In that case, not only are the data samples within one sequence temporally related, but the data samples of different sequences must also be so.

As for the storage of continuous-medium data, the main source of jitter comes from the access time of rotating disk technologies. The sustainable data rate of a magnetic disk is limited as much by the seek and rotational latency as by the platter data transfer rate. More important, the variation in access time depends on the layout of data on disk. In conventional file systems, access time variation is never a deciding factor of data placement. Therefore, it is unlikely that the access time variation is bounded to a level suitable for supporting continuous-media. The problem is compounded by the need to support multiple presentations at the same time. The interference from other presentations, if uncontrolled, can exacerbate the access time variation.

The size of continuous-medium data is another problem. For instance, at 44.1 kHz sampling rate and 16 bits per sample, compact disc (CD) quality digital stereo sound consumes roughly 10 Mbytes of storage per minute (171 Kbytes per second). The figure for video is even more staggering. For instance, when digitised at NTSC TV quality, i.e. 512x480 pix-

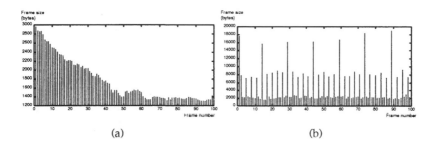

(a)   (b)

Figure 2.1: **Sample frame-size-profiles of MPEG.** The figures show the size of consecutive
frames in two MPEG video sequences. Figure (a) is the profile of a computer graphics ani-
mation. The sequence only contains I-frames which are the compressed images of complete
frames. The frame size varies with the complexity of the picture. Figure (b) is the profile of a
scenery shot. The sequence contains I-frames interleaved with B- and P-frames. As B- and
P-frames are the delta-encoding of I-frames, they are much smaller in size. Hence, the profile
is more bursty than (a).

els, 8 bits per pixel for colour and hue and 30 frames per second, the data rate is over 7
Mbytes per second. HDTV quality video would require a much higher data rate. Clearly,
continuous-medium data have to be compressed before transmission or storage on disks.
Compressed digital video is by nature bursty (figure 2.1). With delta-encoding, which is
used in most video compression standards, there is typically a large spike followed by
smaller frames of motion changes. The allocation of (disk) bandwidth to match the bursty
nature of compressed video is a problem.

Editing of continuous-medium data may need extra storage service support. For instance, voice data are stored as *ropes* in the voice storage server of the Etherphone System
[TS87]. Each rope is implemented internally as lists of pointers to immutable voice record-
ings. The server supports editing operations, such as cut and paste, on *ropes* by manipu-
lating the pointers. The purpose is to minimise the amount of copying involved in editing.
It is true that, by today's standard, the size of main memory available is often enough to
store an entire voice message and editing can be done entirely in memory like ordinary
text data. However, video and HiFi audio can still be too voluminous to handle entirely
in main memory and it can be too time consuming to copy during editing. Therefore, a
level of indirection between the media data and the user-level abstraction, like the *rope*,
seems an appropriate way to minimise copying.

The proliferation of digital video standards presents another problem to continuous-
medium data storage. As Liebhold [LH91] points out, there are a number of digital video
standards, some for full-bandwidth video and some for compressed representations (CD-
I [Inc89], DVI [Lut91], JPEG [Wal91] [CH91], MPEG [Gal91], px64 [Lio91]). The variety
of formats means that the timing information necessary for the timely delivery of data is
encoded in different ways. It is a challenge to design a storage service that can cope with
this diversity.

The topic of continuous-media is an active area of research. The nature of continuous-
media presents a challenge to different disciplines. This work focusses on the impact of

continuous-media on the design of a storage service. The problems raised in this section regarding the storage of continuous-medium data will be addressed in a later part of this dissertation.

2.5 Support of Structured Data

Structured data are objects which consist of component objects. The components may be structured themselves and may be stored separately and referenced from the parent object by name.

A multi-media document is an example of structured data. It is a composition of different information media, such as text, graphics, audio and video. Each component may be stored as a distinct entity and referenced by a "shell" object. Also, the information regarding the presentation order of the various media components has to be stored separately and is likely to be structured as well.

A list of records, whether each record is fixed or variable length, is another example of structured data. A lot of information in real life is record oriented. Not surprisingly, much of the data stored as conventional unstructured files, for instance electronic mail folders, are in fact lists of variable length records. Similarly, the persistent data of database programming systems are structured as well.

A structured object has to be converted from its volatile representation in memory into a suitable form for storage and vice versa. The storage representation should contain sufficient information so that all component objects can be retrieved and reconstructed in memory. The conversion between memory and storage representation can be quite involved if the object structure is complex. If the size of a component is variable and becomes too large to fit into its existing slot, extra space has to be allocated for it. This may not be an easy task especially when the size of the structured object makes it very expensive to overwrite the object entirely when a component is changed.

The Unix file system does not support structured data. Other file systems, such as IBM's ISAM (Indexed Sequential Access Method), may have the notion of records (and a key searching capability). However they do not support variable size records or embedded references to other files. This leaves the applications to invent their own schemes to store structured data.

A question relevant to this work is whether a storage service should support structured data directly. There are several potential advantages of direct support:

1. The structure of the data is itself information that would otherwise be hard to represent.

2. The chance of applications misinterpreting the structure of a piece of data is reduced.

3. The storage service may take advantage of knowledge about the structure of data to improve performance.

4. The storage service can keep track of object references inside structured objects, and detect and remove unreachable objects.

Sue Thomson's work [Tho90] on structured data storage is directly related to this dissertation. She proposes a High Level Storage Service (HLSS) to store structured data. HLSS has two primitive types (byte sequence and object identifier) and a small set of constructors (sequence, record and union). The intention is to support primitive types that correspond to the smallest intended unit of storage access. The task of HLSS is to provide efficient storage access while leaving the fine granularity sub-object organisation to the applications.

The detailed design of structured data storage is not a primary concern in this work. However, the architectural framework proposed in this dissertation incorporates structured data storage as an integral part of the storage service.

2.6   Extensions to the Primary Storage Function

The primary function of MSSA is to store named objects persistently. This section discusses two examples of enhancing this primary function by value-adding clients.

2.6.1   File Indexing

As the volume of data stored in a file system increases, it becomes increasingly difficult to locate the data item one wants. In relation to this problem, some researchers [Sal91] [Sat91] have suggested that it will be very useful to extend the file system by adding associative search or indexing functions. An interesting piece of work in this area is the semantic file system by Gifford et al. [GJSJ91], which provides associative access to attributes extracted from the contents of files.

Many tools exist for associative search and indexing. A simple example is the UNIX command "grep" which searches for the occurrence of some regular expression in some files. However, the semantic file system is special in several aspects. Firstly, it provides automatic extraction of attributes from files with file type specific *transducers*. *Transducers* are programs that understand the content of files and are capable of extracting *useful* attributes from the files. Secondly, the *transducers* work behind the normal file interface and react to changes to files. Therefore, applications and users can access files as before and automatically obtain the additional benefit of associative access to the attributes collected by the transducers. Finally, it overloads the directory tree with the query facility. A query is composed into a directory path name and the result is obtained by listing the directory. The researchers claim that overloading the directory tree with query semantics can improve system uniformity and utility.

The semantic file system has been built from a Unix file system overlaid by a file server process (figure 2.2). The file server process exports an NFS interface. File content attribute queries, in the guise of directory look-ups, are trapped by the file server process. Normal file traffic goes through unchanged to the Unix file system. However, the file server process records file modification events in a write-behind log. An indexing process examines this log and responds to a modification event by re-indexing a file with the appropriate transducer.

Automatic extraction of attributes from files and the associative access to these attributes is an area which deserves more thorough investigation than can be afforded in the time and scope of this work. However, this area of work illustrates the need to extend a storage service by *adding value* to the core function of the service which is to provide long term data storage. The semantic file system work points to the idea of extracting file

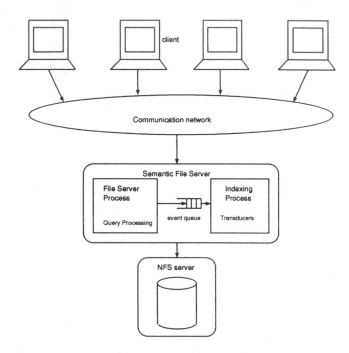

Figure 2.2: Automatic Attribute Extraction in a Semantic File System.

content attributes behind a file interface. This idea is appealing because the attribute extraction process is transparent and unobtrusive, and many applications can easily benefit without any changes to their code.

2.6.2 Persistent Programming Languages

PC++ [ZMB93] is a persistent programming language developed to work with HLSS [Tho90]. It uses HLSS for storing both data and metadata. Also it supports the HLSS object identifier as a special type and persistent class declarations can include HLSS object identifiers. Therefore the application programmer may construct and manipulate object data structures whose components are separately stored objects.

PC++ supports atomic data types and (distributed) transactions. It uses the data structuring capability of HLSS to manage data transfer and shadow versions at the sub-object level. This allows applications to work with very large objects. Also it stores the metadata table which maps its own object identifiers to HLSS object identifiers as a HLSS object. This ensures that the garbage collection function of HLSS can provide the necessary existence control function for its objects even when there are multiple shadow versions of a (sub)object associated with current transactions.

The work on PC++, especially its integration with HLSS, raises the possibility that, with an appropriate storage service interface, clients can implement sophisticated functions over the service and without wasting effort on duplicating the functions already provided.

This work examines an architectural framework to extend the core storage function by

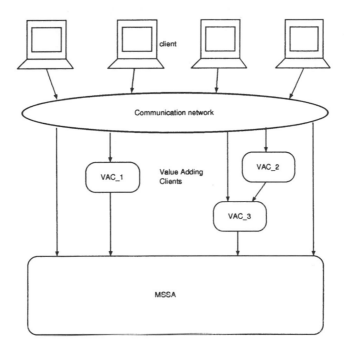

Figure 2.3: MSSA Value-Adding Clients. The arrows in the diagram indicate the client-server relationship. Notice that value-adding clients can themselves be servers to other value-adding
clients.

value-adding clients[2] overlaid on top of MSSA (figure 2.3). Automatic attribute extraction
from files is one example of this kind of service. PC++ is another. The emphasis is on modularity such that new services can be added without affecting existing ones. For instance,
the *transducers* described above could be added as overlay services on top of the MSSA flat
file service. Some files may be piped through the appropriate *value-adding* clients before
they are stored in MSSA whereas others can be stored directly in MSSA if there is no need
to pass through any intermediary.

2.7   Better Data Placement Strategies

Most distributed file systems provide location transparent access to files. The name of a
file in these systems does not reveal where it is stored. In practice, most of the systems
provide *location transparency* by a static mapping from user-level names to server and device locations. However, these systems do not support *location independence* (figure 2.4).
Location independence [LS90] is a stronger transparency requirement— the name of a file
does not change if it is moved from one location to another. This property is essential if
the applications are not to be affected by server directed file movement.

As the scale of network storage systems increases and new media technologies are deployed, there are more options on where to place data. Within the current framework of

---

[2] These services are MSSA clients but they are servers themselves.

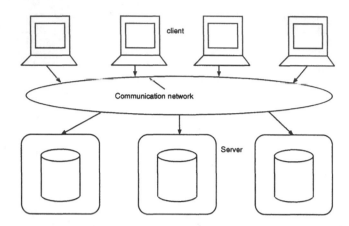

Figure 2.4: Location Dependency of Distributed File Systems. Each file server functions independently. The logical names of files are often statically mapped to physical storage devices.

distributed file systems, users control where data are physically stored by naming the files. The user level names are overloaded with the data placement function. This could be in direct conflict with the users' logical views of data organisation. Also, this rules out any storage resource optimisation that could be done by the storage systems. This is what Gelb [Gel89] characterises as *user-managed storage*, i.e. users have too little information and too much control.

Gelb advocates another mode of storage management which he calls *system-managed storage*. One of the basic principles of *system-managed storage* is the separation of the logical and physical views of storage. The logical domain pertains to the management of data and concerns the characteristics that are intrinsic to the data. The physical domain concerns the utilisation of storage devices.

Wilkes and State [WS91] propose a similar conceptual framework to allow users to specify data availability requirements in a device and location independent way. The storage systems are responsible for matching the requirements with the appropriate storage strategy. Buck and Coyne [BRAC91] propose a distributed storage system that supports transparent data migration in a storage hierarchy consisting of disk, robotic tape (or WORM jukeboxes) and human operated tape vaults. The work emphasizes dynamic specification of file migration paths. The system provides a number of migration paths which can be selected by the users to fit their needs. The actual data placement is transparent to the users.

This work recognises that a storage system is in a better position than the users to decide what types of devices to use and where to put data. The present method of placing data by naming it will not be suitable in a future environment where multiple devices, such as single spindle disks, RAIDs, and optical jukeboxes, with wide ranging characteristics are available. Although automatic data migration is not explored in this work, it is believed that the MSSA architecture, with a clean separation of logical and physical storage functions, will form a good basis to support this advanced function.

2.8 Summary

Contemporary distributed file systems are optimised to store data with certain physical and usage characteristics (section 2.3). *These assumptions are intrinsic in their designs but not explicit at the interfaces.* Moreover, the systems are highly integrated with little room for extension. The lack of extensibility is a significant problem because new data types with very different physical and usage characteristics are being deployed (section 2.4 and 2.5) but the systems are unable to cope; new extensions cannot be added (section 2.6); and new device types cannot be fully exploited (section 2.7). The problem cannot be solved without re-designing the internal structure of a network storage service.

3

Architectural Framework

The purpose of this chapter is to define the architectural framework of MSSA.

3.1 Goals

The previous chapter discussed four areas which existing distributed file systems are not designed to accommodate. The four areas lead to the following four goals which MSSA aims to achieve:

- Support new data types, namely continuous-medium data and structured data, in addition to conventional unstructured data.

- Support the composition of different stored objects, which may be of different types, into composite objects.

- Support the extension of the primary storage functions by value adding services.

- Optimise the utilisation of storage resources and facilitate future extensions to accommodate multiple storage device types.

This work proposes that these goals can be achieved by a divide-and-conquer methodology. Common functionalities are factored into abstractions. And complex abstractions are built on top of more basic ones. The purpose of the architectural framework is to define the division of responsibilities among different abstractions. In later parts of this dissertation, the engineering issues to realise the architecture will be considered.

3.2 MSSA Entities

There are four main entities in the MSSA framework, they are *layer*, *custode*, *container* and *object*. Figure 3.1 shows the relations of these entities. These entities will be introduced in

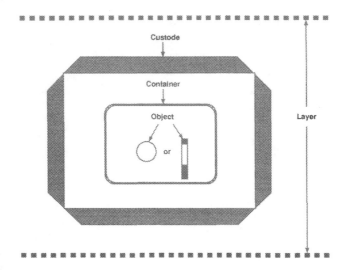

Figure 3.1: MSSA Entities. A Layer consists of custode(s); a custode controls container(s); a container collects object(s).

the later parts of this chapter. Nevertheless, it would be helpful in the understanding of the MSSA framework to bear in mind: a *layer* consists of *custodes*; a *custode* controls *containers* and a *container* collects *objects*.

In this dissertation, the term "object" is used to refer to two basic entities in the MSSA framework, namely *byte segment* and *file*. Unfortunately, the term "object" has been used in the literature to refer to very different things in very different contexts. To avoid any confusion, *object*, *byte segment*, *file* and several other terminologies, which will be used frequently in the dissertation, are defined below. The point to note is that the use of the term "object" here does not imply any sophisticated concepts, such as multiple inheritance and polymorphism, which are common in the object-oriented paradigm.

Entity, Object, Class and Instance

An *entity* is used to refer to any identifiable thing, such as a user, a piece of storage and a process. An *entity* is called an *object* if and only if it is an *instance* of a *class*. A *class* is a type definition and consists of two parts: the interface and the implementation. The interface part describes a set of external operations which provide the only way that clients of the interface can manipulate an *object*. The implementation part describes the internal representation of an *object* and the implementation of each operation. An *instance* of a class is a realization of the class definition. Strictly speaking, a *class* and an *instance* of a class are two separate concepts. Nevertheless, short names, like a "structured file", will be used to refer to an instance of a class (a "structured file class" in this case) unless the context is unclear.

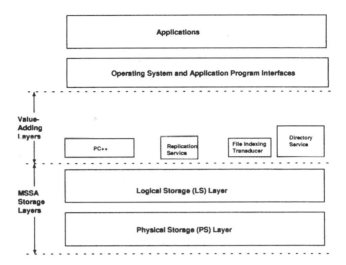

Figure 3.2: **MSSA Layers.** MSSA internally consists of two layers: the physical storage layer and the logical storage layer. The figure also shows some examples of value adding services which are MSSA clients themselves. These services are part of the value-adding layers and not part of the MSSA proper.

Byte Segment

A *byte segment* is an object which represents a piece of permanent storage. They are the basic building blocks for all other objects. Each byte segment is a collection of bytes and each byte is addressable by an integer index starting from 0. The last byte of a byte segment has an index value of (L-1) where L is called the *length* of the byte segment. All integers between 0 and (L-1) inclusively are valid indices. Any integer outside this range is invalid.

File

Files are objects that are created and deleted by MSSA on receiving explicit commands from clients. While conventional file systems only have one file type, there are different file classes in MSSA. Every file is an instance of one file class. Different file classes define different data abstractions, such as unstructured data, structured data and continuous-medium data. The term "file" will be used to refer generally to objects that are stored in the service on behalf of the clients and with additional qualifiers, such as "structured files", to describe stored objects of a particular class.

3.3   Storage Layers

MSSA internally is divided into two layers: the physical storage (PS) layer and the logical storage (LS) layer (figure 3.2). There may be other value-adding layers on top of MSSA but the following discussion concerns the two storage layers within MSSA. The internal structure of the storage layers is shown in figure 3.3.

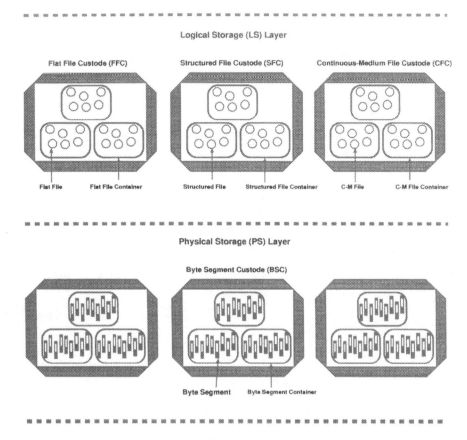

Figure 3.3: MSSA Internal Structure.

3.3.1   Rationale

The reasons for separating the storage functions into two layers are

1. to allow file classes to be developed independently and,

2. to make all the storage resources available in the service accessible to all file classes.

The discussion in the previous chapter has pointed to the fact that the new data types supported by MSSA, such as continuous-medium data and structured data, are fundamentally different from conventional unstructured data. Therefore, it is only natural that these new data types have to be realised within the storage service in different ways.

On the other hand, it is not sensible to implement each file class from "scratch" because a lot of effort will be wasted to "re-invent the wheel". Of course, this concern only arises when there are common functions which are sharable among different file classes.

In this work, the task of managing the data representation on secondary storage is chosen to be the common function shared by all file classes. This is the responsibility of the PS layer. Briefly, the layer provides a versatile data abstraction (*byte segment*) on which different file classes are built. The mechanisms that are related to the data representation are invisible to the upper layer. In particular, the allocation of secondary storage space is dynamic and automatic and is under the control of the PS layer.

This leaves the LS layer to provide the rest of the functions to realise the file classes. In this layer, different file classes are implemented separately. However, the file classes still have to be implemented under a coherent framework. How are files named and located? How are files protected against unauthorised access? How are "lost" files detected and removed? These are issues which are common to all file classes and have to be handled in uniform ways. As one of the goals of this work is to support the composition of different stored objects (or files) into composite objects, this inevitably leads to the need to have cross-references between files. The importance of uniformity becomes more significant as a result.

Another reason to separate the management of data representation on secondary storage into a distinct layer is to make all the storage resources available in the service accessible to all file classes. A storage system in the near future is likely to consist of a variety of storage devices with different characteristics. A separate layer to handle physical storage ensures that the implementations of file classes are device independent and hence can be mapped onto different device types. More importantly, the two layer structure establishes a clear framework on how the placement of data among storage devices of different types is managed by the service. The PS layer controls the physical storage. The LS layer exercises the control on data placement by choosing the places in the PS layer to store file data. The location of file data in the PS layer is invisible at the client level and the LS layer hides any changes in data location from the clients.

3.3.2 PS Layer

The PS layer is responsible for the management of data representation on secondary storage. The layer manages all the storage devices. The devices could be of diverse characteristics, such as single-spindle magnetic disk, RAID and optical jukebox.

The layer provides byte segments where the LS layer can store data. The byte segment interface will be described in section 3.7. There are several important points to note about this layer.

1. *This layer is **only** responsible for the management of data on secondary storage.* A high level and device independent abstraction is chosen as the interface.

2. *There can be different implementations of the byte segment interface.* The implementations may differ because they are based on different storage devices, such as magnetic disks and optical jukeboxes. Also, the implementations may differ because they are optimised to store data with certain physical and usage characteristics. For example, some byte segments are suitable for storing continuous-medium data because they can be accessed at sustained data rates and with jitter controlled; some byte segments can be updated atomically.

3. *The byte segment interface is "requirement-oriented" and does not reveal the implementation details to the upper level.* That is, the upper level distinguishes different implementations with a set of requirement parameters. These parameters may be economy, i.e. cost per unit of storage; reliability and availability; and performance, such as access time and data rate. This also means that different implementations may share

the same storage resource. For instance, an implementation suitable for continuous-medium data may share the same disk with another implementation suitable for normal text data. This facilitates the deployment of storage resource to meet the changing needs of clients.

4. *The same interface is used in all implementations.* The main reason to have a standardised interface is clarity. There is only a small set of concepts and operations which should be easy to comprehend. This is an important consideration in designing a complex system with different parts functioning independently. On the other hand, a standardised interface must allow the right information to flow across it. Also, the interface should be versatile and should not degrade performance significantly.

3.3.3 LS Layer

The LS layer provides MSSA clients with different file classes. Each file class supports a single data type, such as unstructured data, structured data and continuous-medium data. This layer has several important characteristics.

1. *Each file class exports a different interface.* This is necessary because different file classes have different data properties and require different support from the storage service. For instance, the average size of continuous-medium data is too large to "edit-by-copy" and requires direct support from the storage service to minimise copying. On the other hand, text can be handled efficiently by the clients and requires no special storage service support. Moreover, clients must be able to specify the structure of structured data which is not necessary for unstructured data.

2. *Each file class implements all the functions pertinent to the class but the storage of file data must go through the byte segment interface.* All file classes have to map their file data and metadata to byte segments. They also have to provide functions which are class specific. For instance, the file class for unstructured data, which corresponds to the flat files supported by most distributed file systems, must ensure the consistency of data cached by clients. It also has to provide (advisory) locks to coordinate concurrent file accesses. A continuous-medium file class, on the other hand, may not support client caching because the files are too large to fit into client caches or because the locality of reference is poor.

3. *File classes are independent.* Each file class treats the PS layer as a private persistent store. Different file classes do not share byte segments and do not have to coordinate byte segment access with other file classes. However, the byte segments used by different file classes may share storage resource but this is managed by the PS layer and is not visible at the byte segment interface.

4. *File access is location independent.* Each file class may store file data in byte segments that are implemented differently and move the data from one byte segment implementation to another. However, this movement of data is not visible at the file class interface and is transparent to MSSA clients. One reason for moving file data is to exploit the long term locality of file access by moving dormant data to less costly but slower storage media.

It is beyond the scope of this work to present a detailed design of every file class. Nevertheless, it is instructive to highlight what constitutes the logical storage functions of the file classes (or the LS layer). The following is a taxomony of issues in the design of storage services:

Issues	Physical Storage Functions	Logical Storage Functions
Access Control		Yes*
Client Data Caching		Yes
Client-level Naming		Yes*
Client Interface		Yes
Concurrency Control		Yes
Data Integrity	Yes	Yes
Data Migration		Yes
Existence Control		Yes*
Location Transparency		Yes*
Physical Storage	Yes	Yes
* = policy common to all file classes		

It should be quite clear that *physical storage* and *data integrity* are the responsibilities of the PS layer. However, the LS layer also has its share of responsibility because all file data must be mapped on to byte segments.

Notice that, other than *physical storage* and *data integrity*, all the issues listed above have to be dealt with in the LS layer. Moreover, some issues have to be tackled with different policies for different file classes because of the different physical and usage characteristics of the classes. *Client data caching, client interface* and *concurrency control* have been cited in previous discussions as examples that demand different policies. However, there are issues which must be tackled with common policies for all file classes. These include *client-level naming, existence control, location transparency* and *access control*. These issues are independent of the characteristics of different file classes. Moreover, if composite objects are to be constructed by embedding references to other file objects, the files have to be named, located and, when necessary, garbage collected in a uniform way. In the next two chapters, the issues of access control, naming, locating objects and existence control will be discussed in more detail.

3.4 Custodes

Custode, one who has the custody of anything.
Oxford English Dictionary, 1971

The storage layers are composed of custodes which are servers that manage objects (figure 3.3).

Each custode only manages one class of objects. In the PS layer, there are byte segment custodes (BSC) which manage byte segments. In the LS layer, there are flat file custodes (FFC) which manage flat (or byte stream) files; structured file custodes (SFC) which manage structured files; and continuous-medium file custodes (CFC) which manage continuous-medium files.

There are multiple custodes per object class. However, at any time, an object, whether it is a byte segment or a file, is managed by only one custode. In other words, a request to operate on an object must be sent to the custode which manages the object at that time.

Architecturally, the storage service is a distributed entity which consists of a number of custodes. A custode is the smallest unit of distribution. Different custodes may reside on the same machine or be connected by a communication network. The scale of the system is increased by adding more custodes. The state information of objects controlled by custodes can only be obtained by invoking the operations exported by the objects. Other state information, such as where an object is located, is also distributed among the custodes. Furthermore, the distribution model implies that custodes can fail independently. For instance, a BSC can fail while a FFC that communicates with it still functions. Chapter 6 will discuss the issue of independent failure in more detail.

The custode topology in actual implementations is likely to be determined by the hardware configurations. Byte segment custodes must run on the machines which control the storage devices. A file custode can run on any machine and may run on the same machine as the byte segment custode it most frequently communicates with. Custodes running on the same machine may be separated into different protection domains. This may be necessary when some custodes are in their early stages of development and are more likely to crash. Otherwise, custodes on the same machine may be merged into a single address space. This reduces the cost of inter-custode communication to the level of a local procedure call.

If a file custode must communicate with a byte segment custode on another machine to process a file operation, the communication overhead between the custodes would increase the service time of the operation. This work does not address this "performance" problem because this essentially is an implementation issue which depends on the characteristics of the hardware platform. For instance, if the platform is a multi-computer with processing nodes connected by a high speed network and the custodes are distributed among the processing nodes to spread out the workload, the issue becomes a non-problem. Besides, the performance penalty may be tolerable. For instance, the relatively slow device access time to data stored in an optical jukebox may render the communication overhead less significant.

3.5 Containers

So far a level of indirection between objects and custodes has been omitted. The intermediate entities are called containers.

The discussion below applies to both file and byte segment containers.

Conceptually, objects are collected in containers and containers are bound to custodes (figure 3.3). As one can infer from the previous discussion, each container, like the custode it is bound to, can only collect one class of objects. It should be equally obvious that each object belongs to one and only one container.

The functions of containers are as follows.

1. Containers provide the means to locate objects. An object can only be located if the identity of its container is known. If an object migrates from one container to another, the name of the object can remain the same but the subsequent access must

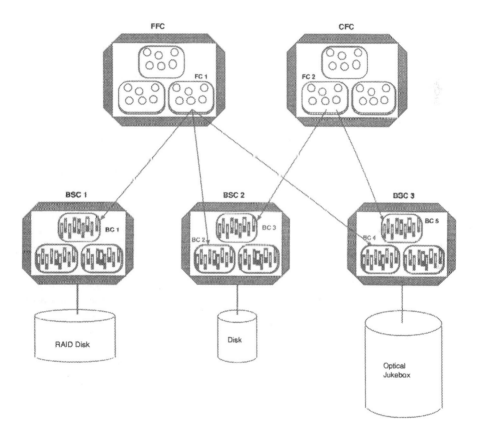

Figure 3.4: MSSA Container Mapping. Related file containers and byte segment containers are connected by arrows.

be directed to the recipient container. As the bindings of containers to custodes are rarely changed, the task of resolving a container identifier to a custode address is quite straightforward. For instance, the mapping from containers to custodes can be stored in a registration server and queried when a container identifier has to be resolved.

2. File containers provide the means to group together logically related files, such as those belonging to the same user, the same group or the same system library. These groupings are natural cost centres for accounting purposes.

3. Byte segment containers differentiate the various implementations (section 3.3). A byte segment custode may control different kinds of storage devices or implement different strategies to optimise for certain physical and usage characteristics. For instance, in figure 3.4, byte segment container "BC 1" is implemented on a RAID disk while "BC 4" is implemented on an optical jukebox. The byte segment custode may export different byte segment containers to encapsulate various implementations. For instance, byte segment container "BC 3" and "BC 2" in figure 3.4 are both controlled by byte segment custode "BSC 2" but the former is suitable for continuous-medium data and the latter is for text and binary. Byte segments collected in the same container would have the same characteristics associated with the container. The file custodes, which belong to the LS layer, can make use of the knowledge of the container characteristics to decide where to put file data.

3.6 Mapping

Section 3.3 pointed out that file objects map to byte segment objects. In fact, file containers map to byte segment containers as well. The relationships among custodes, containers and objects are described below.

Every file container maps to a set of byte segment containers. The reason for a one-to-many mapping is to allow files be stored as byte segments that are implemented differently. The byte segment containers encapsulate different byte segment implementations, such as different storage device types. This mapping is static and determined by the system administrator when the file container is created. For instance, in figure 3.4, flat file container "FC 1" is mapped to byte segment containers "BC 1" (on "BSC 1"), "BC 2" (on "BSC 2") and "BC 4" (on "BSC 3"). Similarly, continuous-medium file container "FC 2" is mapped to byte segment container "BC 3" and "BC 4".

In contrast, every byte segment container is only associated with one file container. Therefore, it is safe to assume that all byte segments in a byte segment container contain the file data or metadata of one file container. If some byte segments in a container are corrupted, it is relatively easy to identify which file container is affected and the extent of the damage this corruption has caused.

A file collected in a file container maps to some byte segments in the set of byte segment containers this file container maps to. However, the file data may be moved among the byte segment containers while the file still logically resides in the same file container. This allows the LS layer to take advantage of the different byte segment implementations to fit the usage and physical characteristics of files. Also, the movement is transparent to MSSA clients because the file container, in which the file resides, remains unchanged.

Containers are bound to custodes. A container-custode binding can be changed under the control of the system administrator, but this should occur infrequently. Objects are bound to custodes indirectly through containers, i.e. the movement of an object from one container to another may require the relocation of an object to another custode.

3.7 The Byte Segment Abstraction

In previous sections, all the main components of the architecture were introduced. In this and the next sections, the interface between the PS and LS layer is examined.

This section describes the byte segment abstraction exported by the PS layer. The next section introduces BSC sessions. BSC sessions allow performance requirements on byte segment accesses to be specified. The byte segment abstraction and the idea of BSC sessions are closely related. Both, in turn, are related to the division of responsibilities between the PS and LS layer (or between the file and byte segment custodes) as laid down in the framework.

3.7.1 Data Abstraction

A byte segment is a sequence of bytes. The minimum unit of access is a single byte. When a byte segment is created, it is zero in length. Subsequently, the length of the byte segment is extended as data are written to it.

The data abstraction is chosen at a level high enough to encapsulate all the mechanisms that deal with data organisation on storage devices. Disk blocks are allocated to store a byte segment as it is extended. Externally, byte segments are (logically) continuous sequences while, internally, the disk blocks allocated to store a byte segment may not be contiguous. The translation from a byte segment offset to a disk block address is not visible outside the byte segment abstraction.

3.7.2 Operations

A basic set of operations is provided to create, delete and access byte segments. The exact interface is defined below. Readers not interested in the fine details may skip to the end of this section.

bs_create [containerID] → [status, byteSegmentID]

> Create a byte segment in the byte segment container identified by containerID.

bs_delete [containerID, byteSegmentID] → [status]

> Delete the byte segment identified by byteSegmentID in container containerID.

bs_write [containerID, byteSegmentID, index, size, data] → [status]

> Write data into the region starting at offset index to index + size - 1 inclusively. The length of the byte segment is increased to index + size - 1 if its value before the operation is smaller than this value. Data can be written in any order. In particular, if index is larger than the current length of the byte segment, an *uninitialised* fragment is formed between the old and the new fragments.

bs_read [containerID, byteSegmentID, index, size] → [status, count, data]

> Read data from the region starting at offset index to index + size - 1 inclusively. The value of count returns the number of bytes read.

> The semantics of reading an *uninitialised* fragment is implementation dependent. Reading an *uninitialised* fragment may be reported as an error. This is arguably good semantics because the act of reading data which have not yet been written before may be an indication of incorrect program behaviour and should be trapped. On the other hand, the on-disk representation of byte segments may not be suitable to keep track of *uninitialised* fragments, especially when they are not aligned on disk block boundaries. Alternatively, *uninitialised* fragments may be filled automatically with some default pattern and no exception is raised when reading the fragments. This semantics is fairly straightforward to implement but is weaker than the former approach because a program error which results in the reading of uninitialised data may not be detected. The former approach can always emulate the latter if necessary but not vice versa. Chapter 6 describes a BSC design that traps the reading of *uninitialised* fragments.

> So the value of count returned may be less than the value of size under two conditions. Firstly, the region specified may extend beyond the current length of the byte segment. In this case the bytes between offset index and the end of the byte segment are returned. Secondly, some implementation may report an error when the read starts within an *uninitialised* fragment. The value of count returns the smaller of the two values: the size of the *uninitialised* fragment counting from offset index or the value of size. Also, in an implementation which traps the reading of *uninitialised* fragments, if the read starts within a data fragment but extends into an *uninitialised* fragment, only the bytes in the data fragment are returned.

bs_getlength [containerID, byteSegmentID] → [status, length]

> Return the current length of the byte segment.

bs_setlength [containerID, byteSegmentID, length] → [status]

> Set the length of the byte segment. If the value of argument length is larger than the current length of the byte segment, an *uninitialised* fragment is formed between the old and the new length of the byte segment.

An important characteristic of the byte segment abstraction, which may not be obvious from the description above, is that all byte segments are removed by the PS layer **only** when the bs_delete operation is invoked by the LS layer. In other words, the LS layer is responsible for removing any byte segments which do not contain any valid data. In order to delete any garbage byte segments, the LS layer must first know of their existence. A special operation is provided to allow the LS layer to obtain a list of all the byte segments currently collected in a byte segment container. Each list appears to the LS layer as a byte segment with a special byteSegmentID and can be read with the bs_read operation. From the list, the LS layer is expected to identify any garbage byte segments and delete them accordingly. This process can be done in conjunction with garbage collection at the file level because the two are closely related.

3.8 BSC Sessions and Tickets

3.8.1 Rationale

One of the main characteristics of the MSSA framework is the encapsulation of different storage device types and storage organisations by a single abstraction— the byte segment. The idea of a uniform interface for all implementations is appealing because it is a good design practice to work with a minimum set of concepts and interfaces.

However, one must balance the uniformity of the byte segment interface against the requirements of **different** file classes. Every file class only relies on the PS layer to provide byte segments for storing file data. It has to provide the rest of the class functions. Continuous-medium data have stringent temporal requirements which must be met to ensure an acceptable presentation quality. As various stages on the data path between the storage device and the media input/output device must cooperate to fulfill the temporal requirements, the temporal characteristics of accesses to byte segments storing the data must be well defined. Hence, the continuous-medium file class has special byte segment access requirements that are not applicable to others. However, the file class only requires temporal performance guarantees during real-time presentations. Other data accesses, such as for image processing or voice recognition, do not have any temporal requirements.

The temporal characteristics of continuous-medium data do not make the byte segment abstraction unsuitable for this data type. The special characteristics do imply that special performance requirements have to be met during real-time presentations. These performance requirements are not needed for other byte segment accesses.

Rather than using **ad hoc** measures to cope with the special requirements of continuous-medium data, the idea of **BSC** *sessions* is introduced. This provides a generic mechanism to specify performance requirements on byte segment accesses.

3.8.2 Session Interactions

A BSC session is a sequence of byte segment accesses which are associated with certain performance requirements. Potentially, there can be different kinds of BSC sessions, for which different performance requirements can be specified. However, this work only investigates one kind of BSC session, i.e. the *rate-based* sessions which provide the performance guarantee necessary to support continuous-medium data. *Rate-based* sessions will be discussed in detail in chapter 8.

Notice that BSC sessions are **not** mandatory to byte segment accesses. In other words, it is necessary to establish a BSC session only when there is a need to specify certain performance requirements, as is the case with the real time presentation of continuous-medium data. All byte segment accesses which are not associated with sessions are handled in the standard (or default) way.

A BSC session has to be established and withdrawn explicitly using the BSC session interface. These actions are orthogonal to byte segment accesses. The interface to establish a session is as follows:

open_session [containerID, byteSegmentID, ticketAttribute] → [ticketID]

The byte segment to which the session applies is specified in the arguments.

The performance requirements are defined in the argument ticketAttribute. The content of this argument depends on the type of sessions. A ticket (ticketID) is returned and will be used to identify a session in subsequent byte segment accesses.

A session may be established to cover more than one byte segment. This can be achieved using the following interface:

open_group_session [byteSegmentList, ticketAttribute] → [ticketList]

The argument byteSegmentList specifies a list of byte segments and a list of tickets is generated, one for each byte segment. This list is returned in ticketList.

Byte segment accesses that are associated with sessions are invoked as follows:

write_bs [containerID, ticketID, index, size, data] → [status]
read_bs [containerID, ticketID, index, size] → [status, count, data]

The byte segment operations— write_bs and read_bs — are overloaded to perform session and non-session accesses. The ticketID shares the same format as the byteSegmentID. This argument identifies the byte segment to which the access is targeted and the BSC session the access is associated with.

Finally, a session can be closed with this operation:

close_session [ticketID, sessionArg] → [status]

The argument sessionArg contains session specific information.

Notice that the performance requirements are specified when a session is established and will cover all the byte segment accesses associated with the session. This eliminates the need to evaluate the performance requirement on a per access basis. However, there is a more important reason for fixing the performance requirements when a session is established.

The purpose of having BSC sessions is to **guarantee** (at least at a high probability) that the performance requirements defined for the sessions are met. The performance guarantees inevitably mean that resources have to be committed to meet the requirements. The need to commit resources, which are finite, to sessions implies that eventually the spare resources remaining may not be sufficient to meet the requirements of new sessions. The ways to handle these overload situations depend very much on what the performance requirements are. However, fixing the performance requirements when a BSC session is established allows the BSC to evaluate the requirements against the resources available and to turn down, if necessary, the session requests when the requirements cannot be met.

This completes an introduction to the idea of BSC sessions. The topic will be returned to in chapter 8 when the idea of *rate-based* sessions is discussed.

3.9   Related Work

Now that the ideas behind the MSSA framework have been described it is appropriate to compare it to other multi-layer storage systems.

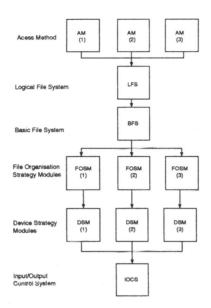

Figure 3.5: Generalised File System Model.

3.9.1 Modular File System Design

The idea of building sophisticated file systems in multiple layers of abstraction is not new. Madnick and Alsop [MA69] defines a generalised file system model with six hierarchical layers shown (in simplified form) in figure 3.5. It is a framework for describing the structure of file systems. In the middle of the hierarchy is the *basic file system*. This provides a sequence of blocks abstraction. Above this layer is the *logical file system* which associates a textual name to a file. The next layer up is a set of *access methods* which superimpose a number of formats, such as sequential fixed-length records and sequential variable-length records, on the basic file abstraction. The *basic file system* can be implemented on top of a number of device dependent methods. Each method uses a different way to map a logical address within a file to a disk block (*file organisation strategy module*), and a different way to allocate disk blocks and schedule I/O operations (*device strategy modules*).

There are similarities between the MSSA framework and this model. The PS layer corresponds to the *basic file system* and the layers below. The LS layer corresponds to the *access method* layer though the function of the LS layer is more than just imposing a format on a universal file system. The *logical file system* layer roughly corresponds to the directory server external to MSSA. The different byte segment implementations correspond to different stacks of *file organisation and device strategy* modules. However, the model does not have the concept of value-adding clients. It is a model for centralised systems and cannot describe the distribution of functional entities.

3.9.2 HLSS and LLSS

The High Level Storage Service (HLSS) and the Low Level Storage Service (LLSS) are results of the Ph.D. work done in the Computer Laboratory by Sue Thomson [Tho90] and

Tim Wilson [Wil92b] respectively.

HLSS has been briefly described in section 2.5. It is a general purpose storage service for storing structured data. The service was designed to work on top of LLSS.

LLSS is a general purpose flat file server. It was designed to exploit non-volatile RAM to permit faster writing. Although HLSS is one of its clients, it was designed to support other clients just like a conventional file server. The LLSS interface supports file access control (in the form of capabilities) and locking but does not provide any file attributes other than the size of a file.

Much of the experience with HLSS can be applied to the design of the SFC. The BSC performs a similar role as LLSS. However, most of the LLSS functions, such as file access control and locking are not present in the BSC. This is because they are considered to be file class dependent functions and should be performed at the LS layer. MSSA also addresses other architectural issues such as naming, object location and protection in a broader context than HLSS and LLSS. The use of non-volatile RAM in storage services is also considered in the design of a BSC which will be discussed in chapter 6.

3.9.3 DataMesh

DataMesh [Wil89] [Wil92a] is a research project on network storage service. The target hardware is an array of processing nodes interconnected by a fast, reliable, small area network. The nodes serve different functions. Some provide network connectivity; some control disks, an optical jukebox or robot tape library; and some have (volatile or non-volatile) RAM for caching, read-ahead, and write-behind. The project's emphasis is on the exploitation of parallelism available from the underlying hardware.

The software architecture consists of three layers. From top to bottom, they are *file access methods*, *chunk-vector managers* and *virtual devices*. The *virtual devices* supply *slots* where data can be stored. A slot may be constructed from one or more physical storage elements; can potentially be replicated; and can be migrated to and from a tertiary store. The *chunk-vector managers* supply chunk vectors which are sequences of contiguously-addressed *chunks*. A *chunk* is a piece of storage built from *slots* and has a fixed size over its lifetime. There are chunks of different sizes. The *file access methods* provide different application-visible objects with byte- or record-level interfaces.

The project is in its first phase of work which is mainly concerned with the *virtual devices* layer. The underlying theme is to investigate smart placement of data on disk to improve disk throughput using new disk request scheduling, disk shuffling, fast-write disk, decentralised RAID 5 and other device optimisation techniques.

MSSA is similar to the DataMesh software architecture in that the LS layer roughly corresponds to the *file access methods* and the PS layer corresponds to the *chunk-vector managers* and *virtual devices* combined. Nevertheless the emphasis is different. MSSA is concerned with the interaction of the two layers to provide support for different file types. The work done in the PS layer, which will be described in chapter 6 and 8, is more concerned with providing the right quality of service to the LS layer than with maximising the device throughput. DataMesh, at the moment, concentrates on improving disk throughput and very little has been reported on the interaction between the higher and lower layers.

3.10 Summary

This chapter identified the four goals of this work. A multi-layer storage architecture was introduced.

A two layer structure within MSSA is chosen in order to achieve two of the goals set forth at the beginning of this chapter, i.e. the support of new data types and the optimal utilisation of multiple storage device types. The PS layer provides a common basis on which different file classes can be developed separately in the LS layer. Device dependency is confined to the PS layer. Hence, files can be mapped onto different device types and even migrated, as necessary, among the devices available.

The temporal requirements of continuous-medium data highlights the need to specify performance requirements dynamically at the byte segment interface. The idea of BSC sessions is introduced to provide a generic mechanism to specify performance requirements on byte segment accesses.

This chapter gave a board outline of the architectural framework. In the rest of this dissertation, a number of issues arise from this framework are considered.

4

Access control

The purpose of access control is to decide who is authorised to have what access rights to which objects. In general, there are three aspects to access control in (distributed) systems. *Protection* is to prevent a client from accessing a server object that it shouldn't. The protection of objects depends on *authorisation*, which specifies the access rights of subjects to objects. *Authentication* is to verify the identity of a subject, for whom a client acts as an agent, so that the server can decide whether an object may be accessed.

This chapter starts with a discussion on the protection requirements in MSSA (section 4.1). There are two ways to represent authorisation information: access control lists and capabilities. Neither of them alone is sufficient to fulfill the protection requirements. Section 4.2 introduces the two mechanisms and highlights their strength and weakness. After that, the rest of this chapter discusses the method to perform access control in MSSA. The method combines access control lists and capabilities to exploit the strength of both mechanisms.

4.1 Protection Requirements

In MSSA, file custodes protect files from unauthorised client accesses. In the following, a distinction is made between *end-clients* which are agents of human users, such as programs running on workstations, and *value-adding clients* which are services that extend the functions provided by MSSA. A *network service*, such as a print server, may also be a client of a file custode when it has to access files controlled by the custode. Figure 4.1 shows the variety of client access paths.

Obviously, *end-clients* should only have access to files for which they are authorised. Equally, a service provider, such as a *value-adding client* or a *network service*, should be restricted to have access only to the data that are needed to perform the service and only for the duration of the service. This requirement, commonly referred to as the *least privilege* principle [SS75], is essential in limiting the amount of damage a faulty service provider (or one which has been compromised in security) can cause.

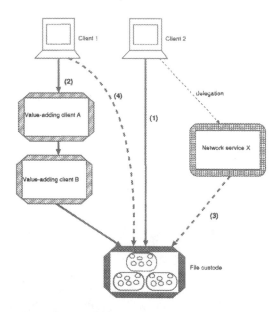

Figure 4.1: Access Paths. *End-clients* can access files: (1) directly; or (2) indirectly through *value-adding clients* which have control over the files. (3) An *end-client* may delegate a *network service* the right to access a file. The *network service* normally doesn't have the necessary privilege. (4) The *value-adding client(s)* which controls a file may temporarily grant an *end-client* the right to access the file directly instead of going via the *value-adding client(s)*.

Normally, *end-clients* which access files indirectly through *value-adding clients* should not be allowed to by-pass the *value-adding clients*. For instance, *end-clients* should access directories through a directory server (a *value-adding client*) and should not be allowed to access the files containing the directory data directly.

However, there are situations in which a *value-adding client* has to grant **end-clients** the rights to access files **directly**. A multi-media database is an example of such a *value-adding client*. Consider a hypothetical multi-media database which manages a large collection of data items of different media, such as text, graphics, audio and video. The database stores these data items as files in MSSA. In response to a query from an *end-client*, the database has to find all the relevant data items and to report the result to the client. However, the database cannot simply return the data by value; it is not practical with non-text data items, such as audio or video clips. Instead, the database returns a list of identifiers which point to the files that contain the relevant data. On receiving the result of the query, the *end-client* may choose to read a video file listed in the result. The *end-client* can put the request to the database which in turn reads the file and ships the data to the *end-client*. However, this is rather inefficient and undesirable because it complicates the design of the database. Instead, the database can **grant** the **end-client** the right to **read** the file **directly**. In doing so the database no longer has to participate in the data transfer. To minimise the misuse of information, the database must have jurisdiction over the transfer of the access right to the end-client. Also, it must be able to revoke this access right after the client has finished reading the file.

The transfer of an access right may go in the other direction. Consider a *network service*, e.g. a print server, which takes a file as a parameter. An *end-client*, which wants to use the print server, must be able to pass the file to the service. If one excludes the often impossible method of shipping the whole file to the service, the preferred way of interfacing is to pass the file by reference and let the print server access the file directly. According to the *least privilege* principle, the print server should not have general access rights to all files. Therefore, an acceptable solution would be to temporarily pass the access right for the file to the print server but only for the duration of the service.

4.2   Authorisation

The access matrix

In order to control access to files, the file custodes need to know the access rights of clients to these files. Conceptually, this information can be represented by an access matrix [Lam74]. In the matrix, the rows represent the subjects and the columns represent the objects. The access rights that a subject holds for an object can be found at the intersection of the corresponding row and column.

In this discussion, the files are the objects to which access is controlled. A subject in the matrix can be a user so that any agent that speaks for the user is granted access. A subject can be a service provided by a *value-adding client* or other service providers. For clarity, the term **principal** will be used to refer to either a user or a service. A group of principals can be considered jointly as a subject so that the rights defined for this subject are enjoyed by all the principals which comprise it. In the following, the term **subject** will be used to refer to either a principal or a group when no distinction between the two is necessary.

Such a matrix is too sparse to be stored in its entirety. In practice, the information contained in the access matrix is represented in more compact forms that can be retrieved easily when needed.

Access control lists (ACL)

A column of the access matrix describes all the subjects that have access to an object. It is the access control list (ACL) for the object. It can be attached to the object and checked when an access is requested. For a given object, it is possible to efficiently determine which subjects are allowed access. Revocation of access rights can be done inexpensively. On the other hand, checking access privilege can be slow. Propagating access rights from one subject to another can be difficult to express.

Capabilities

An alternative way to represent the access matrix is to have each principal associated with a list of objects it has rights to access. Each element in the list is a *capability* [DH66]. When an access is requested by a principal, the capability is presented to verify that the access right does exist. Capabilities are like tickets in real life. A theatre ticket alone is a sufficient proof of the right to watch a performance.

Because only the validity of capabilities has to be verified, authorisation checks can be performed more efficiently with capabilities than with access control lists. It is also easier to transfer access rights with capabilities. Capabilities can be copied and passed on to other principals and they can be restricted before being passed on. On the other hand, it is not easy to find out which principals have capabilities to an object. Revocation of capabilities is difficult, especially when only some of the capabilities for an object should be revoked and not the others. This is because capabilities can be copied and stored freely, thus it is impractical to locate and invalidate all the revoked copies.

Capabilities must be unforgeable. If object identifiers are chosen from a very large set of numbers and there is no practical way to deduce an identifier by guessing or by testing with randomly generated patterns, these identifiers may be used as capabilities. The Cambridge file server [Dio80] use this form of identifier as file capabilities. However, the access right associated with such an identifier cannot be further restricted. Hence, it is not suitable for passing on to other principals if the principal holding the capability wants to limit their individual rights. Alternately, a capability can be made unforgeable by attaching a signature to the capability. The signature is generated by passing the other contents of the capability and a secret number held by the server through a one-way function. Any tampered-with or forged capabilities would have wrong signatures. Amoeba [ASTvR86] is an example that uses this form of capabilities.

In a distributed environment, servers cannot control where capabilities are stored and how and to whom they are copied. A malicious intruder can intercept all the data packets on an Ethernet and copy capabilities from these packets. In other words, the propagation of capabilities can neither be controlled nor traced by the servers. Gong [Gon89] proposes the *identity-based capability* scheme which allows servers to limit the propagation of capabilities. The identity of the principal that can use a capability is embedded in the capability. The capability is made unforgeable in a similar way as the Amoeba scheme. When a capability is presented to the server, the identity of the client is authenticated and only if it speaks for the principal embedded in the capability will the access be granted. When a principal wants to pass on a capability to another principal, the server is contacted for a new capability to be generated. This gives the server the opportunity to enforce a security policy and to reject the request if necessary.

4.3 Authentication

Authorisation check depends on the ability of a server to authenticate its clients. The principal on whose behalf a client works for must be known for an ACL check. An *identity-based capability* must be checked against the principal a client speaks for. Authentication in distributed systems is accomplished using encryption-based protocols, such as those described by Needham and Schroeder [NS78] or implemented in Kerberos [SNS88]. The following discussion assumes that an authentication mechanism is available for file custodes to authenticate clients.

Having described the three aspects of access control, the method to perform access control in MSSA can be discussed.

4.4   Access control in MSSA

The following describes the mechanisms to perform access control in MSSA. They are the result of collaborative work[1]. Basically, MSSA uses ACLs to represent authorisation information. However, temporary capabilities are used for access checking.

Capabilities provide a simpler mechanism to transfer access rights temporarily. This flexibility is useful in MSSA, for instance, to allow a *value-adding client* to transfer access rights to an *end-client* (section 4.1). Capabilities are also easier to check. On the other hand, ACLs give a more rigid form of control, in which the extent of access can be reviewed and changed with relative ease. The combined use of ACLs and capabilities is intended to exploit the advantages of both approaches to provide a flexible way to perform access control.

From the information stored in ACLs, capabilities are generated and used in file accesses. In addition, a principal holding a capability is allowed to ask for "special" capabilities for other principals. These "special" capabilities differ from those capabilities generated from ACLs in that their access rights are not recorded in the ACLs. However, their presence in the ACLs are implicit because the principals that ask for the "special" capabilities can either insert the access information explicitly or act as the intermediary for them. With the "special" capabilities, the temporary transfer of access rights is simplified because there is no need to modify ACLs explicitly.

The format of the capabilities is derived from Gong's *identity-based capability* (section 4.2), i.e. each capability is only usable by one principal. They are only valid for limited periods of time. In other words, they are not intended to be stashed in files for later use. The rationale behind this decision will be discussed in section 4.6.

4.5   The Use of Access Control Lists in MSSA

File accesses are controlled by the information stored in ACLs. Each container is associated with an ACL— the *container ACL*. This ACL provides coarse grain access control on all files in a container. Optionally, each file can be associated with a separate ACL— the *file ACL*. This ACL complements the container ACL by allowing fine grain access control at a per file level. The use of these ACLs is described below.

Container ACL

Each file **container** is associated with an ACL. This list defines the principals (and/or groups) that can:

- **create** new files in the container;
- modify this ACL;
- modify any file[2] ACLs in the container;
- read any file[2] in the container;
- write any file[2] in the container; etc.

---

[1]The requirements and the combined use of ACLs and capabilities are my own work. The details of the mechanisms are the product of collaboration with Richard Hayton.

[2]Subject to further restrictions applied to individual file

The container ACL represents access control information that applies to all the files in the container. The principals (and group names) in the container ACL can have all or part of these rights.

At the minimum, a container ACL is needed to define who is allowed to **create** files in the container. When most of the files in a container share the same access right setting, the container ACL provides an efficient way to represent these rights. This compact representation has another benefit:

Conceptually, clients have to acquire a capability for each file in order to perform future accesses (section 4.5). These capabilities have to be cached in the client domains and could consume a significant amount of storage space. The generation of new capabilities adds overhead to file accesses (though this performance cost can be amortised over a number of future accesses). Container ACLs can help to reduce the need to generate new capabilities. A capability generated from a container ACL can be used to access all the files in the container that are not restricted by individual file ACLs (see below). If most of the files in a container do not have per-file ACLs, a substantial saving can be achieved because all the capabilities that would have been generated can be replaced by a single capability.

Value-adding clients are most likely to benefit from the compact representation of access control information. Consider a directory server which stores all its directories as (structured) files in a container. A single entry in the container ACL is sufficient to give the directory server the necessary right to all the files in the container. The directory server only needs to hold one capability to gain access to all the files. The files are probably protected from other clients. Any clients that want to access the directories must go through the directory server.

In general, logically related files are likely to share the same access right setting. System binaries and library files are publicly readable. A user who is concerned with privacy is likely to protect most of her files from other users. Alternately, a user may allow all her files to be read by others except for a few private files, such as electronic mail folders. As the division of files into containers is intended to reflect the logical relations of files (section 3.5), container ACLs are likely to be a compact way to represent the access rights for these files. Of course, there would be files in containers that require different access right settings, the *file ACLs* are to cater for these exceptions. Nevertheless, container ACLs allow for effective access check optimisation when possible and do not have any undesirable effect when such a coarse grain control of access is not sufficient.

File ACL

Container ACLs provide a coarse grain control of access. This may not be sufficient for some applications. Therefore, each **file** can also be associated with an ACL. However, unlike the container ACL, this ACL is **optional** and need only be defined for those files that require the finer grain of control. The file ACL defines the principals (and/or groups) that have access right to the file. The access rights are the same as listed above except the create right which is only applicable to container ACLs. The relation of a container ACL and a file ACL is as follows:

- If a file ACL is not defined for a file, the access rights of a principal to the file is determined by the container ACL. The total rights the principal inherited from the ACL are the union of all the rights collectively specified for the principal and for all the groups of which the principal is a member.

- If a file ACL is defined for a file, the access rights of a principal to the file is the union of the rights the principal inherited from the file and the container ACL. For example, a user can read a file if she is in the container ACL but not in the file ACL. Similarly, the user can read a file even if she is only in the file ACL.

Negative rights

With *positive rights* alone, a principal on the container ACL will have the rights to all the files in the container. This is not satisfactory because a user may want to protect sensitive files selectively but allow wider access to all other files by default. Of course, this kind of selective protection can be achieved by attaching to every file an ACL to control the file's access and not having any principal other than the user on the container ACL. However, this is not an efficient way to represent the user's intention, which is to consider the (presumably small) set of sensitive files an exception rather than the norm.

Instead, MSSA uses *negative rights* included in ACLs to indicate the denial of the specific rights. Negative rights take precedence over positive rights. Titan [BFH+67] allows a file owner to deny a particular principal the access right while permitting other principals to access the file. The same idea has been used in Andrew [SHN+85] to provide a rapid way to deny a principal the access rights to a large set of files. This is necessary in a large distributed system, such as Andrew, because revocation information, such as the removal of a principal from a group, may take time to propagate. Negative rights can reduce the window of vulnerability since changes to ACLs take effect immediately. For this purpose, negative rights can be included in a container ACL.

Negative rights can be included in ACLs of selective files to override any rights a principal might have inherited from the container ACL. For instance, specifying negative rights for *other* principals not specified in a file ACL would have the effect of denying any principal, other than those on the file ACL, the access rights.

4.6 The Use of Capabilities in MSSA

Capabilities are passed in file operations for access checking. These capabilities could be generated directly from the information stored in container or file ACLs. They could be generated following requests from clients with the appropriate capabilities. The newly generated capabilities can be used to transfer access rights to other principals not on the ACLs. The transfer of access rights with capabilities will be explained in the later part of this section.

Capability format

The capability format is shown in figure 4.2. A capability can only be used by the principal identified in the capability. Hence an intruder cannot gain access to a file with a stolen capability unless she can falsify her identity as well. The bit-fields, F and rights, encode the access rights associated with the capability. A client can insert any bit-pattern in the

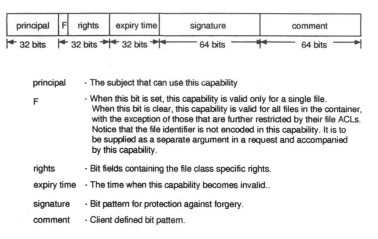

principal	F	rights	expiry time	signature	comment

|◄─ 32 bits ─►|◄─ 32 bits ─►|◄─ 32 bits ─►|◄──────── 64 bits ────────►|◄──────── 64 bits ────────►|

principal	- The subject that can use this capability
F	- When this bit is set, this capability is valid only for a single file. When this bit is clear, this capability is valid for all files in the container, with the exception of those that are further restricted by their file ACLs. Notice that the file identifier is not encoded in this capability. It is to be supplied as a separate argument in a request and accompanied by this capability.
rights	- Bit fields containing the file class specific rights.
expiry time	- The time when this capability becomes invalid..
signature	- Bit pattern for protection against forgery.
comment	- Client defined bit pattern.

Figure 4.2: Capability format.

comment field (or it can just be filled with zeros). This field is **not** interpreted by the file custode but, like other fields in the capability, it is protected from tampering. The purpose is to allow clients to seal in extra protection information when necessary. (An example will be given later to illustrate the use of this field.)

A capability is valid until the expiry time. With a 32-bit field, the expiry time can conveniently contain the time in units of seconds, for instance, the number of seconds since midnight January 1, 1970 GMT, which is widely used in UNIX systems to represent time values[3].

Scope of capabilities

A capability may carry the access rights to a single file, in which case the F-bit (figure 4.2) is set. Alternatively a capability may carry the right to create files in a container and/or the rights to access the files in the container, in which case the F bit is cleared. In other words, the *scope* of a capability could be a single file or a single container. Because a capability may be used to access more than one file, there is no file identifier embedded in the capability. The necessary container identifier and file identifier must be supplied as separate arguments in file accesses.

A per-container capability can be viewed as an automatic entry in a container ACL (section 4.5). In fact, the per-container capability may be generated directly from the information stored in the container ACL (see the descriptions below). Similarly, a per-file capability is an automatic entry in a file ACL. A problem arises when one uses a per-container capability to access a file with an individual file ACL. (File ACLs are optional. Those files without an individual ACL are protected by the container ACL. There is no problem in using a per-container capability to access these files.) This is a problem because the file ACL

---

[3]There is, of course, an implicit assumption that the clocks on different systems are well synchronised. This is a reasonable assumption in today's networking environment where clock synchronisation protocols, such as the Network Time Protocol, can maintain the accuracy of system clocks to a few tens of milliseconds over a wide area [Mil90].

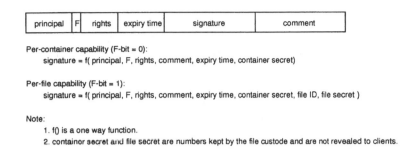

| principal | F | rights | expiry time | signature | comment |

Per-container capability (F-bit = 0):
    signature = f(principal, F, rights, comment, expiry time, container secret)

Per-file capability (F-bit = 1):
    signature = f(principal, F, rights, comment, expiry time, container secret, file ID, file secret)

Note:
    1. f() is a one way function.
    2. container secret and file secret are numbers kept by the file custode and are not revealed to clients.

Figure 4.3: Making Capabilities Unforgeable. The signature field of a capability is generated by passing the rest of the capability and the secret number(s) held by the file custode through a one-way function. When the capability is presented later, the expected signature is computed in the same way as outlined and is compared with the value embedded in the capability. Any tampered-with capability would have the wrong signature. Notice that the file custode only needs to keep the the secret numbers and not the complete copy of the capability. Each container has one *container secret* and each file has one *file secret*.

may contain negative rights that override the access rights sealed in the per-container capability. Hence, the access should not be granted without first checking the file ACL.

One solution is to reject such a request whenever a file is found to have a file ACL. The client is told of the possibility that the access may be granted if it re-tries with a per-file capability. The client should proceed to acquire such a capability, possibly by using the rights it inherits from the per-container capability. This approach is chosen in the present design because it has the advantage of speed of response and requires minimal work on the part of the file custode. On the other hand, requests may be rejected when they should not have been and this causes unnecessary disruption to client activities.

Another solution is to check the file ACL to see if there is any conflict. This is not desirable because one of the reasons for using capabilities is to avoid checking ACLs in file accesses. However, the extra effort on the part of the file custode does eliminate the negative effect of unnecessary rejections.

Other hybrid solutions are possible. A flag can be stored in a file's metadata and is set when the file's ACL contains negative rights. As the access rights of a per-container capability can only be overruled by negative rights, it is safe to proceed if the flag is clear. If the flag is set, the request can be rejected and the client has to acquire a per-file capability. Another solution is to perform an ACL check on first access and return to the client a per-file capability which it should use in subsequent accesses. Clearly, the solutions represent different tradeoffs between performance and client transparency.

Generating capabilities

A client can request a new capability with the grant_capability operation. The interface looks like this:

        grant_capability [origCap, containerID, fileID, principal, F, rights, comment,
                        expiryTime] → [status, newCap]

If, after performing the necessary access check the file custode decides to grant the designated principal a new capability, it fills in the capability with the information supplied and a *signature* number. The *signature* protects the capability from tampering and is computed as shown in figure 4.3.

The capability argument origCap is optional. If the capability is present, it contains the access rights the calling client is holding. If this is a valid capability, the file custode would accept the request. Of course, the requested rights can only be equal to or a subset of the rights contained in origCap. Otherwise, any principals could acquire more rights than they should have by asking for new capabilities for themselves.

If the argument origCap is omitted (or filled with an agreed pattern to indicate that its content is invalid), the file custode interprets this as a request to generate a new capability from the information stored in the ACLs. The request is checked in the following way:

- If the request is for a per-container capability (F-bit = 0), the container ACL is consulted to see if the designated principal has the necessary rights.

- If the request is for a per-file capability (F-bit = 1), the container ACL and the file's ACL, if it exists, are consulted to see if the designated principal has the necessary rights.

The details on how the file custode determines the rights of the principal from the ACLs were described in section 4.5. One has to be a bit more careful if origCap is a per-container capability and the request is to generate a per-file capability. The file's ACL, if it exists, must also be checked to ensure that the rights of origCap are not overruled by the negative rights of the file ACL.

The client may ask for more access rights than the file custode is prepared to give. Instead of rejecting the request, the file custode just generates a new capability with the subset of the requested rights that has passed the access check. This is a useful policy because it allows the client to skip a redundant query to find out from the ACLs what access rights a principal possesses.

Temporary transfer of access rights

Having described how capabilities are generated, it is now appropriate to look at the temporary transfer of access rights from one principal to another using capabilities. Basically, any principal with a valid capability can transfer all or part of the access rights by asking for a new capability for the other principal.

A user who can read a file can print the file by asking for a read capability for the print server and giving the print server the capability. The print server can then read the file from the file custode directly. The example multi-media database discussed in section 4.1 can give the *end-client* a read capability so that it can read the video file directly. There is no need to manipulate any access control list. Since a capability is automatically revoked after its expiry time, the originator can choose to forget about the capability with the full confidence that it will not remain valid indefinitely.

Notice that **any** principal with a valid capability is allowed to pass on the access rights to another principal. This is really a policy decision rather than anything intrinsic in the mechanism. The file custode can implement a different policy and restrict the transfer of access rights by rejecting the grant-capability requests that do not conform with the policy. However, in a distributed environment, it is not clear why putting more restrictions on "who can transfer what rights to whom" is in any way more secure. If the originator has the right to modify the file ACL (or the container ACL), he can always insert the recipient of the capability into the list. Even if the originator is not allowed to modify the file ACL, he can still pass on the content of the file, instead of the file reference, to the recipient. The file custode has no jurisdiction over what the originator can do in the client domain. Stopping the originator from passing on his access rights with capabilities does not prevent him from giving away the file data. This only makes the transfer of data less convenient, which is exactly what the use of capabilities is trying to overcome.

Revocation of capabilities

Capabilities are revoked automatically when they reach their expiry times. Capabilities can also be revoked immediately by simply changing the secret numbers held by the file custode. Changing the *file secret number* (figure 4.2) would revoke all the capabilities associated with the file. Similarly, changing the *container secret number* would revoke all the (per-container and per-file) capabilities associated with the container. Undoubtedly, the revocation mechanism is rather draconic. It is not possible to revoke capabilities for a file immediately and **selectively**.

However, capability revocation is known to be a difficult problem. Gong [Gon89] proposes a revocation mechanism that requires an exception list be associated with an object. Revoked capabilities for an object are stored in the exception list. In an access, both the validity of the capability and the exception list are checked to prevent the use of revoked capabilities. Apart from the logistic difficulties of storing such a variable length list, this list can never be removed without performing full revocation. But it is not clear how full revocation can be performed without affecting the capabilities that should remain valid.

As the expiry time already provides a means to revoke most capabilities automatically, it is safe to assume that full revocation is only required very infrequently. There is very little work the file custode has to do to perform capability revocation. Full revocation provides a fall-back mechanism to revoke any capability that might pose a security risk. For example, when the rights of a principal are removed from a file ACL, the capability that has been issued to this principal should be revoked. Moreover, any capabilities that the principal has passed on to other principals should also be revoked. Full revocation provides the means to do this. On the other hand, clients must be ready to refresh their capabilities that have been affected by full revocation. This may not be possible if the capabilities originally come from other clients that have since gone off-line. Nevertheless, one does not know, without putting the system into practice, whether this problem is merely an inconvenience or whether it is intolerable. As a starting point and in the absence of a better alternative, the approach is an attractive compromise.

Using the comment field

The comment field in a capability allows the client to seal in additional protection information into the capability.

Consider a directory server as an example. For the sake of consistency with the file

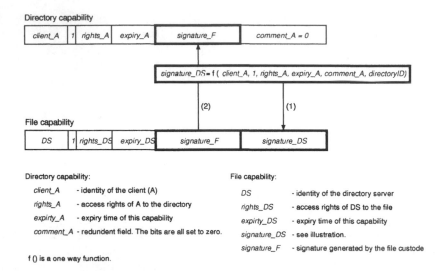

Figure 4.4: **Using the comment field.** This example illustrates how the comment field can be used to seal in additional protection information. A directory is stored as a file. The capability for the directory is generated from the capability for the underlying file. The directory server first computes *signature_DS*. This number is passed to the file custode as a comment. The file custode returns a file capability with this comment sealed in. The signature of the file capability (*signature_F*) is then used as the signature of the directory capability. Notice that the directory server does not need to maintain any secret data or to keep a copy of the file capability. When the client presents the directory capability subsequently, the file capability is regenerated and is validated with the file custode. Any tampered-with directory capability would be detected because the file capability derived from it would be invalid.

interface, the directory server has to provide the same access control mechanisms as the file custodes. Directories have ACLs and capabilities are used for access checking. Directory capabilities could be generated in the same way as file capabilities. In other words, the directory server could keep the secret numbers for the directories and generate directory capabilities in the same way as file capabilities. However, this would require the directory server to manage data that have to be kept secret. Moreover, the secret data have to be stored, like other directory data, in files. Because the secret data must be protected from being stolen off the network, the data have to be encrypted before leaving the directory server.

By using a one-way function and the comment field, the directory server can generate capabilities and does not need to manage any secret data. The details are shown in fig 4.4. A directory capability is derived from an underlying file capability. The directory server does not need to store the directory capability or the file capability. When a directory capability is presented by a client, the directory server can validate the capability by reconstructing the file capability and asking the file custode to verify that the file capability is valid.

This way of generating capabilities can be extended to multiple layers. Each layer can seal in its access information into the comment field that is passed down to the next layer.

No secret has to be kept in the layers. However, all the layers have to be consulted to validate a capability at the top layer. This access check can be performed in conjunction with a data access. For instance, the directory server has to read directory data from files. It can verify a directory capability by using the file capability derived from the former to access the file that stores the directory data. If the file access is denied, the directory server can deduce that the directory capability is not valid.

4.7 Summary

This chapter considered the protection requirements in MSSA. The temporary transfer of access rights is useful to allow clients to transfer data securely and conveniently. An access control mechanism, which can provide this kind of flexibility, was presented. ACLs are used to represent authorisation information and temporary capabilities are used for access checking. The design takes advantage of ACLs to provide a more rigid form of control while using capabilities to facilitate the temporary transfer of access rights.

5

Naming and Related Issues

In this chapter, the issue of naming is addressed. The problem with file existence control is defined.

The issue of naming in MSSA is fairly straight forward. Nevertheless, the multi-layer characteristic of the architecture calls for careful considerations. Names have to be given to objects at each layer and these names have to be resolved to some other names at a lower layer. Multi-layer naming could be a source of inefficiency, because there may be too many name look-ups; or unreliability, because there may be too many places these look-ups could fail. This chapter looks at how these problems can be minimised.

5.1   Textual Names vs Identifiers

Files in conventional file systems are often given textual names and organised into hierarchical directories. Some operating systems, such as Plan 9 [PPTT90], go a step further and name all devices and other non-file entities just like real files.

The main appeal of this "everything has a path name" approach is simplicity. Users only have to deal with a single naming concept. If names are chosen carefully, they could even convey certain clues to the content of the files. On the other hand, it may be difficult to give some files meaningful textual names, such as e-mail messages in a mail queue. For these data items, file names only provide unique identifiers and do not convey any other meaning.

The issue MSSA has to address is not whether textual naming is useful. It is essential for human users to be able to name files textually. The question is whether the storage service should have an integrated directory tree.

This work chooses to name all files and byte segments with identifiers, which are fixed-length bit patterns. The task of providing a directory tree is left to some MSSA client. These clients are likely to be servers themselves. Using identifiers to name stored objects is not new, for instance, the Cambridge File Server (CFS) [Dio80] uses 64-bit UIDs to name files. Nevertheless, there are several considerations that support this choice and not all of them are relevant to previous work:

Service extensibility

Firstly, the immediate clients of the storage service may not be tools directed by users, as in conventional file systems. There may be additional service layers that add value to the primary storage functions of MSSA (section 3.1). A textual name interface is a hindrance to service extensibility.

A database programming system has to convert its objects in memory into suitable forms for persistent storage. A textual name interface at the storage service boundary is not natural for this kind of system as most database programming objects may just be internal locations and do not have ready made textual names.

Functions, such as file indexing, are better added behind the textual name interface in order to be transparent to applications. If path names visible at the application interface are hardwired to the storage service, this kind of service is more difficult to add.

Composite objects

Secondly, MSSA has to support composite objects containing embedded references to other files. These embedded references must be interpretable in a universal context. With textual names, they have to be full path names starting from a common root, assuming that such a root exists. They are of variable length and can be very long. Identifiers, on the other hand, are compact and universal.

Logical view of data organisation

Thirdly, an integrated directory tree does not correspond to a user's logical view of data organisation. MSSA supports different file types by separate custodes. This has the effect of dispersing data items which are logically related at the user level. An example is a multimedia document which is stored separately as files on different custodes. If path names are tied to custodes, these data items would have unrelated textual names. For instance, a video clip of the multimedia document might be named "/video/home/fred/video/flowerclip" while a related annotation text might be named "/text/home/fred/text/flowertext"[1]. This is undesirable because the path names are "contaminated" by the MSSA architecture and do not reflect the user's perspective of logically related data items. With a separate directory service, the user may set up a directory "/home/fred/flowlearn" and this directory may contain the files "flowerclip" and "flowertext".

Object existence

Finally, besides naming, an integrated directory tree defines object existence. A file is kept if and only if its name is in any directory. With embedded file references, the clients might want MSSA to keep a file if its name is embedded in any file. In such an environment, the existence control function of a directory tree breaks down; the idea of object existence has to be redefined.

---

[1] Assume that the user Fred has a continuous-media file container alias to "/video/home/fred" and a flat file container alias to "/text/home/fred".

5.2   Naming

In MSSA, there are two kinds of identifiers. They are *container identifiers* and *object identifiers*. A container identifier, as the qualifier implies, is the name of a container, which can be a file or a byte segment container. An object identifier is the name of a file or a byte segment. Container and object identifiers are different in format and serve different purposes. Their formats and usages are explained below.

Mapping

In this section, the concepts of object and container mappings are frequently referred to. The concepts have been explained in chapter 3. In particular, it is important to understand that file custodes store files on secondary storage via the byte segment interface. So conceptually, files are mapped to byte segments. Also, files are collected in file containers and byte segments are collected in byte segment containers. A file class may utilise different byte segment implementations. So conceptually, a file container is mapped to one or more byte segment containers which encapsulate different byte segment implementations.

5.2.1   Considerations

There are several considerations in the design of container and object identifiers:

Location independence

Container and object identifiers should be location independent because containers and objects may be moved and it is impossible to find and alter all references to them when they are moved. From the point of view of system management, it is necessary to be able to move containers from one custode to another. A container may be moved from a disabled custode to a functioning one. Also, a container may be moved to balance the loading of a group of custodes. As byte segment containers encapsulate various byte segment implementations, a byte segment has to be moved from one container to another to take advantage of the different physical and usage characteristics provided by the containers. Although MSSA does not move files among file containers spontaneously, the provision of location independent file identifiers gives MSSA clients the option to move files among file containers in accordance with their own needs.

Length and format

Container and object identifiers should be fixed-length and have the same format in all layers. Fixed-length identifiers are easier to use in composite objects containing embedded references to other objects because the space allocation of fixed-length data items is easy.

Type information

As different object types have different interfaces, a container identifier should contain the type information of the objects collected in the container. However, one should note that an object identifier does not need to contain type information if the identifier is always accompanied by a container identifier. This is because a container and the objects it collects must be of the same type. Furthermore, if a container identifier contains location information, an object identifier can just be a pure name [Nee93]. A pure name is nothing but a bit-pattern and does not yield any information by examining the name itself. Hence, the only use of an object identifier is for comparing with other bit-patterns for identity.

Multi-layer characteristic

The multi-layer characteristic of MSSA is another consideration. Object identifiers of one layer have to be resolved into identifiers of the next layer. File identifiers have to be resolved into byte segment identifiers. A byte segment identifier has to be resolved into the disk blocks that contain the byte segment. If there are additional value-adding layers above the LS layer, each layer has to resolve the object identifiers in that layer to the identifiers of the lower layer. Perhaps the obvious way to resolve an object identifier in each layer is to look it up in a table. This approach has two drawbacks:

- The look-up tables are vital to the proper functioning of the system. Any damage to the tables is likely to cause the loss of a number of objects. Furthermore, an update to a look-up table must be made carefully so that a crash occurring during the update will not damage the data integrity of the table.

- There is a performance cost in resolving an identifier by table look-up. The size of a look-up table is too large to cache locally in a file custode because there can be tens of thousands of files in a file container. To resolve a file identifier by table look-up, different parts of the table have to be fetched from the PS layer. This raises the performance cost of the resolution process. The same argument can be applied to the value-adding layers.

If table look-up is used to resolve identifiers in every layer, the two problems would multiply in gravity. This is a very undesirable situation. Hence, unnecessary name resolution through table look-up should be avoided at all layers.

Now that the considerations behind the design of container and object identifiers have been described the format of the identifiers can be introduced.

5.2.2   Container and Object Identifiers

Figure 5.1 shows the formats of container and object identifiers. The type field of a container identifier indicates the class of objects stored in the container. A container is uniquely identified by the instance field. All container identifiers have different container instance numbers. So no two containers have the same instance number, even if the containers are of different types.

An object identifier and a ticket (section 3.8.2) share the same format and are both 64-bit numbers. If the most significant bit (T in figure 5.1) is clear, the number is an object identifier. Otherwise, it is a ticket. An object identifier has the following properties:

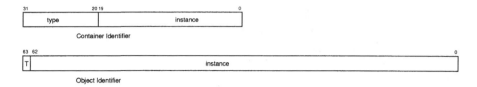

Figure 5.1: The formats of container and object identifiers.

- An object identifier uniquely identifies an object in a class. Hence, an object can be moved from one container to another with no need to change its name.

- An object identifier is never reused even if the object it refers to has ceased to exist. This leaves open the possibility of restoring objects from off-line storage. This is useful because objects may be deleted by accident, caused either by system or user errors. However, this is not the only reason for not reusing object identifiers. The absence of an object in the container where it is created does not necessarily mean that the object has been deleted. It may have been moved to another container. Once an object has moved out of a container, it is difficult to determine whether the object still exists. Therefore, it is unsafe to reuse identifiers.

- Although object identifiers are unique within the same object class, the same bit-pattern may be used as identifiers for objects of different classes. For instance, the bit-pattern of a flat file identifier may be the same as a byte segment identifier. To uniquely identify an object out of the set of all objects, an object identifier has to be supplemented by a container identifier. The container identifier provides the type and location information of the object.

5.2.3 Generating Object Identifiers

The assignment of container identifiers to containers is a system administration procedure. This work assumes that MSSA is administered by a single authority and the authority is responsible for the uniqueness of container identifiers.

Independent identifier generation

Objects can be created simultaneously in containers that are managed by different custodes. It is necessary to ensure that custodes of the same class do not generate the same bit-pattern as identifiers for different objects.

One approach is to choose new bit-patterns randomly. Since the number of patterns in a 64-bit number is much larger than the population of objects, the probability of a random bit-pattern being reused to name different objects is very low. However, there is no absolute certainty that duplication would not occur. Another approach is to embed the identity of the name generation centre in a new bit-pattern. In this way, bit-patterns generated by different name generation centres are guaranteed to be different.

An object identifier must not be reused. One can embed object creation time in identifiers. The monotonic advancement of the real clock guarantees that identifiers are not reused. The robustness of this approach depends on the quality of the clock implementation. If a clock is wrongly set backward, the uniqueness of identifiers cannot be guaranteed. An error which sets a clock forward is also dangerous if a later correction causes the clock to jump backward.

This work uses an epoch number scheme which is well known for its robustness. A new bit-pattern is generated by concatenating the container instance number (20 bits) with an epoch number (43 bits). The container instance number comes from the container where the object is created. The uniqueness of the number guarantees that all bit-patterns generated in this way are different, irrespective of where they are generated. The epoch number is private to the container. After the new bit-pattern is generated, the number is advanced and will never be reset to a smaller value. The epoch number is preserved on secondary storage to guard against it being reset to a smaller value when a system is restarted. The image of the number on secondary storage does not have to be updated whenever the number is increased. The stored value only needs to be larger than the in-memory copy at any time. This can be achieved by updating the stored value in large steps when the in-memory value catches up with the stored value.

Optimisation in multi-layer naming

In theory, object identifiers in all layers can be generated using the scheme described above. However, the resolution of an upper layer to a lower layer identifier in a multi-layer architecture is a problem, in terms of efficiency and reliability. In practice, a file identifier does not have to be a new bit-pattern and can be the same as the byte segment identifier it is supposed to resolve into. This eliminates the need to resolve file identifiers. The detail is explained below.

If a file is represented by a single byte segment and the byte segment is **not** shared with other files, the file identifier can simply be the same bit-pattern as the byte segment identifier. There is no danger of two or more files in the same file class sharing the same bit-pattern as identifiers because the uniqueness of byte segment identifiers guarantees that this situation would not happen.

Notice that the "overloading" of a byte segment identifier into a file identifier is possible because an object identifier is a pure name and does not contain any type or location information. There is also no danger of misinterpretation because file and byte segment identifiers are used in different contexts. File identifiers are used at the file interfaces; byte segment identifiers are used at the byte segment interface.

If a file is mapped to multiple byte segments, the identifier of the "shell" byte segment which contains all the references to other component byte segments can be used as the file identifier.

The "overloading" scheme cannot be applied to files that are stored as parts of a byte segment. A file custode has to generate new bit-patterns as their identifiers. However, the same file custode can still "overload" byte segment identifiers as file identifiers for other files. There is no danger of name collision between the two identifier generation schemes because any new identifier bit-pattern generated in MSSA is guaranteed to be unique.

The "overloading" scheme can be applied across multiple layers. An example is a directory server which needs to name directories with identifiers. Clients can refer to individual directories with no need to specify their full path names, which are long and costly to resolve. Suppose a directory is stored as a structured file. The structured file, in turn, is stored as a byte segment. The structured file identifier can be generated by "overloading" the byte segment identifier. In the same way, the structured file identifier can be assigned as the directory identifier. As structured file identifiers are unique, the directory identifiers would inherit the same property. There is no need for the directory server to generate bit-patterns for its identifiers.

5.2.4 Locating Containers and Objects

From a file identifier, a file custode must be able to determine the identity of the byte segment that represents the file. This is easy with an "overloaded" file identifier because the byte segment identifier is just the same bit-pattern. However a byte segment identifier alone is not enough to locate the byte segment. The file custode still has to determine in which container the byte segment is stored.

The file custode has two pieces of information at hand. It knows in which file container the file is stored. It also knows which byte segment container(s) the file container is mapped to. If the file container is mapped to only one byte segment container, the byte segment must be stored in that container. However, a file container could also be mapped to more than one byte segment containers. In this case, the file custode has to determine in which one of the containers the byte segment is stored.

The simplest approach is to try the containers in turn until the byte segment is located. If the containers reside on different machines, the process can be speeded up by performing the search in parallel. Once the relevant container is determined, this information can be cached in the file custode to avoid repeating the search when the byte segment is accessed again.

The above approach assumes that containers are searched at random. An alternative is to use some heuristics to direct the search. As a byte segment identifier contains the container instance number of the container where the byte segment is created, this information can be used as a hint and that container is contacted first. If byte segments are rarely moved among containers, the byte segments are likely to be in the containers they were created in. When a byte segment is moved to another container, a forward pointer can be left in the original container to point to the new one. A subsequent search can be conducted by following the chain of forward pointers. This further increases the chance of finding the right container in minimal search steps.

Finally, it is fairly straightforward to locate the custode which controls a container. Container identifiers are recorded in a registration service and the service is queried to resolve a container identifier to a custode address. The result of a query is cached locally to avoid further queries when the container is accessed again. The registration service can be replicated to improve service availability.

5.2.5 Naming and Value-Adding Clients

The examples of value-adding clients given in section 2.6, PC++ and file indexing, represent two kinds of value-adding services. PC++ is an example of value-adding services that use MSSA primarily as a persistent store. These services export their own interfaces which do not have any relations with MSSA interfaces. File indexing is another kind of value-adding service. These services differ from the previous ones because they provide new "file" classes that can be used in the same way as files. Although it is beyond the scope of this dissertation to explore all the issues related to value-adding clients, the naming mechanism of MSSA is designed to allow for the two kinds of extensions in the following ways:

Firstly, all MSSA objects are referenced by identifiers, instead of textual names. This simplifies the management of internal names within services like PC++. Moreover, the textual name interface, i.e. the directory tree, can be placed fairly close to the applications. It is possible to insert additional layers between MSSA and the directory tree to create new "file" classes. These new "file" classes can be accessed at the directory level like other MSSA files. This allows services, such as file indexing, to function transparently between applications and MSSA.

Secondly, container and object identifiers are designed to name, in a uniform way, MSSA file classes and new "file" classes provided by value-adding services. New "file" classes can be distinguished from other file classes with new container identifiers. From a container identifier, clients can determine the file type and locate the server, which may be a MSSA custode or a value-adding service, responsible for the files.

A uniform way to name and locate all objects is important. This allows references to new "file" objects to be embedded in composite objects. Also, custodes, such as a SFC, can handle references to new "file" classes without any modification.

5.3   Existence Control

MSSA has to delete unwanted objects to reclaim the storage space used by them. Deletion in itself is simple but the task of deciding when an object becomes disposable is difficult. A file is unreachable if no reference to the file exists in the client domains. In a system with an integrated directory, the task of detecting unreachable files might be difficult, especially with a freely connected directory graph [Sal73]. Nevertheless, the existence of a file can be clearly defined by a system predicate, i.e. a file can be removed if it does not appear in any directory entry.

As a research goal, MSSA must support composite objects which contain references to other objects. It is obvious that MSSA should never discard any components of a composite object unless it has received explicit commands from clients. In other words, if a composite object contains a reference to a file, the file should be considered reachable. However, the problem is recursive because the parent object may not be reachable itself. Clearly, there must be some predicate to test for reachability, This could be difficult to define if references can be freely embedded in files to form composite objects. Even if this can be defined, testing this predicate can be difficult. Embedded references to files on another custode may have to be verified with the custode. The custode may not be accessible at that moment.

The issue of existence control will not be addressed in this dissertation. Current work in the Computer Laboratory includes an investigation to solve this problem based on periodic refreshing [BMTW91].

5.4 Summary

This chapter gave the reasons for choosing identifiers, instead of textual names, to name files. Identifiers are generated in a uniform way. They are fixed-length, location independent and suitable for embedding in composite objects. Resolving names in multiple layers is a problem specific to MSSA. The container and object identifiers are designed to reduce the cost of multi-layer name resolution.

6

The Design of a Byte Segment Custode

6.1 Introduction

This chapter describes the design of a byte segment custode (BSC). The main characteristic of this design is that all byte segment operations are atomic. A transaction facility is built around a non-volatile RAM buffer to support the execution of byte segment operations. NVRAM has been deployed for some years to improve the *write performance* of file servers. The use of NVRAM in this work is different from others because the aim of this work is to use NVRAM to provide better *write semantics* at high performance. Also, the implementation has achieved a very short crash recovery time as a result of using NVRAM with transactions.

The reasons for the use of NVRAM and the support of atomic byte segment operations are discussed in section 6.2. The rest of this chapter describes the design in detail.

6.2 Design Considerations

6.2.1 Failure Recovery

One major design issue of any storage service is how to recover from failures. That is, a system must be able to recover to a consistent state after it fails and restarts subsequently. If the behaviour of a system is characterised by its invariants, these invariants must evaluate to true when the system is in a consistent state. An operation that transforms a system from a consistent state to another consistent state has to be executed as a sequence of actions. A system failure can interrupt the execution of such a sequence at arbitrary points. Therefore a system that has just restarted after a failure may not be in a consistent state. It can roll forward to a new consistent state by resuming the execution of operations that have been interrupted. It can also roll back to a previous consistent state by undoing actions that have been completed. Moreover, a system that recovers by rolling back to a previous consistent state may do so by undoing some operations that have been completed and positively acknowledged. File systems, such as the (re-implemented) Cedar [Hag87] file system, Episode [CAK+92], JFS [CMR+90] and Sprite LFS [RO91], that use the logging [Gra79] technique to maintain consistency, are examples that exhibit this kind of behaviour. This is because the tail of the logs in these systems are kept in volatile memory and are lost when the systems fail.

Although the undoing of previously acknowledged operations can recover a system to a consistent state, it is questionable whether this technique is suitable for a distributed environment where clients and file servers can fail independently. The clients would have to detect and put right any loss of data as a result of a server failure. I believe this is a wrong way to apportion responsibilities because the loss of data is purely an artefact of the way the server is implemented. This may be justified in the short term on the ground of performance, such as the amortisation of disk access latency with large transfers. It is not a forward looking solution, especially when non-volatile RAM is becoming a viable addition, both technically and economically, to the storage hierarchy.

6.2.2   Failure Recovery in MSSA

In MSSA, the issue of recovery is added a new dimension by the separation of storage functions into two distinct layers. The reason to divide the storage service into different layers and processing entities (custodes) is to establish a framework to divide a complex system into different components that can be designed independently. The success of this modular approach depends on finding the right interfaces that are efficient to use and can minimise undesirable interference between different components. Applying this principle to recovery, it follows that all custodes, file and byte segment custodes alike, should recover by taking independent action and with as little coordination with other custodes as possible. Furthermore, this work assumes that custodes can fail independently because they can be running on different machines. For example, a BSC can fail while a SFC that needs to communicate with it still functions. In this case, the subsequent recovery of the BSC should have little or no impact on the functioning of the SFC.

In terms of failure recovery, this BSC design offers the best semantics because the BSC behaves like an ideal system. Every byte segment operation that has been completed and acknowledged would persist across shut-downs and failures. Any operation that has been interrupted by a failure is guaranteed to have no effect at all after the custode recovers. The BSC does not need to coordinate with other custodes in the recovery process. Conversely, other custodes that interact with the BSC do not need to take any actions other than to invoke the interrupted operations again.

6.2.3   NVRAM and Atomic Updates

The performance cost of atomic updates can be high. Early work [Dio80] [FO81] [BKT85] [SMI80] that investigates transaction support in network file systems all extract a high performance cost in exchange for atomicity. In contrast, this design has the potential to achieve high performance because it has made several design trade-offs. These trade-offs are discussed below.

Use of NVRAM

NVRAM has been used as fast write back buffers for some time. For instance, the IBM 3990 disk controller [MH88] has NVRAM built-in; NFS accelerators, such as Prestoserve [MSC+90], use NVRAM to buffer synchronous NFS write operations. In these examples, NVRAM is put behind the disk driver interface. This ensures that the devices are compatible with existing file systems and minimum modification is needed to harness the performance advantage of non-volatile memory. Solid state memory is orders of magnitude faster than magnetic disk. The performance of a storage system can increase dramatically when the disk subsystem is coupled with a NVRAM buffer that is large enough to absorb bursts of I/O operations. At present, there is a 10-20 times difference in price between the cost of a megabyte of magnetic disk memory and a megabyte of dynamic memory. Also, the cost of a battery backup system to maintain the content of the memory when conventional power fails can be substantial. (A 600VA UPS with enough power to support a DEC-station 5000 for one to two hours costs about £500). In addition, the use of battery back-up to achieve non-volatility has two drawbacks. It is difficult to verify that the batteries will be fully charged when needed; and it is difficult to determine how long the NVRAM must be made to persist. Nevertheless, the cost of RAM is decreasing rapidly and the engineering difficulties are not insurmountable. Hence, this work assumes that NVRAM is a viable addition to the storage hierarchy in the near future. ([CKKS89] argued in 1989 that NVRAM has already been cost-effective for most applications.) The question is how to exploit the speed and random access characteristics of NVRAM. The approach taken by this design is to use NVRAM as a write back buffer as well as the basis of an internal transaction facility to support byte segment operations.

Update size limitation

An atomic update must be smaller than the size of the non-volatile memory available. An immediate consequence of this decision is that no redundant information is needed to be kept on disk to process an update. This greatly simplify the underlying mechanism to support atomicity. On the other hand, this is an obvious limitation but provided that the size of the NVRAM buffer is large, this limitation should not be a serious problem.

Single operation atomicity

In this design, atomicity only encases a single byte segment operation. This avoids the complexity of supporting transactions that span multiple operations. Traditionally, transaction mechanisms are used to ensure consistency in the presence of concurrency and failures. In MSSA, concurrency control is not necessary at the byte segment interface because file custodes are responsible for coordinating byte segment accesses. On the other hand, it might be useful to group together multiple updates to a byte segment into a single transaction. This is because file custodes may need to perform multiple updates per file operation. Supporting multiple update atomicity could further simplify the file custodes' task of error recovery. Externally, these transactions can be identified by BSC sessions. Although multiple update atomicity is not investigated in this work, the underlying mechanism to support atomic updates can be extended in future to support this feature.

Having discussed the reasons for the **use of non-volatile memory** and the **support of atomic byte segment operations**, the rest of this chapter will discuss the design in detail.

6.3 NVRAM Transactions

The BSC performs all **updates** as transactions. These transactions are called NVRAM transactions because they are performed using a NVRAM buffer.

Eswaran et al. [EGLT76], define a transaction as a sequence of actions which, when executed, transform a system from a consistent state into a new consistent state. If the actions are classified as either read or write, the system has to guarantee that after recovery from a system crash, for each transaction, either **all** of the write actions will have been executed, or **none** will have been. This is usually called the atomic property of transactions.

A common technique to implement the all-or-nothing property of transactions is called the two-phase commit [Gra79]. The central idea behind any two-phase commit algorithm is that a transaction is made atomic by performing it in two phases. One implementation of (non-distributed) two phase commit is to record updates in intention lists:

Phase 1 The information necessary to do the write transactions is recorded in a series of intentions, without changing the data stored by the system. The transaction can be aborted (i.e. none of the changes will be seen by any other transactions) and any modification undone by discarding the series of intentions. If the transaction is to proceed to completion, the last action of this phase is to *commit* the transaction which has the effect of making it no longer possible to abort.

Phase 2 The changes recorded in the intentions are applied to the actual data.

If a crash occurs after the transaction commits, but before the second phase is finished, the second phase is restarted. This restart could occur as many times as necessary to complete the transaction. This requires the intentions to be idempotent, i.e. executing the same intention multiple times would have the same effect as if it is executed once. Alternatively, the system must be able to detect, by inspecting the target data, whether the intention has already been carried out.

Furthermore, the atomicity of the transaction depends on the *commit* action being atomic. This is the point at which the change takes place from a state in which it is still possible to abort the transaction to one in which the changes must be made permanent, despite subsequent system failures.

6.3.1 Overview

Every byte segment operation that **writes data** to disk blocks is executed as a NVRAM **transaction**. A NVRAM transaction is a sequence of updates to disk blocks that are cached in the NVRAM buffer. Before a transaction commits, all the updates are recorded in an intention list which is also stored in the NVRAM buffer. The *commit* action is accomplished by setting a bit in the intention list. After a transaction commits, its intention list is processed and the changes recorded in the list are written to the cached copies of the disk blocks involved in the transaction. These cached blocks are then put onto a write-back disk queue. When all the intention records are processed, the space occupied by the intention list is freed for other use.

The non-volatile property of the NVRAM buffer guarantees that the data stored in the buffer would persist across system failures. The intention lists of the transactions that are in progress when the BSC crashes are retained in the NVRAM buffer. The recovery process only has to determine the state of the NVRAM buffer before the crash and complete all committed transactions.

The transaction facility depends on the NVRAM buffer being byte addressable by the processor (as will be explained). It is also assumed that updating a byte in the NVRAM buffer is atomic and a crash due to software or hardware errors would not corrupt the content of the buffer.

6.3.2 NVRAM Buffer Blocks

Before the transaction facility is described, it is necessary to understand how the NVRAM buffer is organised. The NVRAM buffer, which is a continuous memory segment with battery back-up, is divided into fixed size buffer units, called *buffer blocks*. Each buffer block is the same size as a disk block which is 1 Kbytes in the prototype. The organisation of the NVRAM buffer is shown in figure 6.1.

A buffer block can be used either to cache a disk block or to store records of a transaction's intention list. Hence, a buffer block can be in one of the three states:

FREE The buffer block does not contain any valid data.

DATA The buffer block contains a valid copy of a disk block.

INTENTION The buffer block contains some intention records of a transaction.

The state of a buffer block is recorded in a *buffer block descriptor* which is stored in a reserved region of the NVRAM buffer. The content of a buffer block descriptor is shown in figure 6.1. The descriptors contain sufficient information to allow the BSC to determine the state of buffer blocks when the custode restarts. If a buffer block is in the *DATA* state, the descriptor contains the device and disk block number of the cached disk block. If a buffer block is in the *INTENTION* state, the descriptor contains a transaction identifier and sequence number. Buffer blocks that contain intention records of a transaction are tagged with the same transaction identifier and ordered according to the sequence numbers.

The state transitions of buffer blocks must be atomic, otherwise a crash during a state transition would leave the buffer block in an ambiguous state. On the other hand, changing all the fields of a descriptor would require multiple memory store instructions and cannot be guaranteed to complete atomically. Therefore, the valid state transitions (figure 6.2) must be restricted to those which can be accomplished by a single memory store instruction, i.e. those that change to or from the *FREE* state. This is because only the *state* field of a descriptor needs to be changed in these transitions and can be performed by a single memory store instruction.

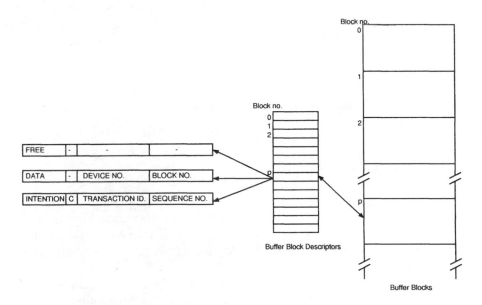

Figure 6.1: The Organisation of the NVRAM Buffer.

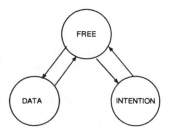

Figure 6.2: Valid State Transitions of a NVRAM Buffer Block.

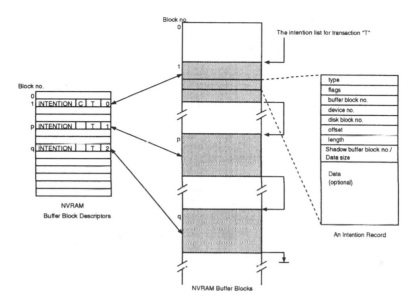

Figure 6.3: The Intention List of a Transaction.

6.3.3 Intention Lists

The intention list of a transaction is stored as NVRAM buffer blocks (figure 6.3). The identifier of the transaction is recorded in the descriptors of these blocks. Each descriptor also contains a sequence number which determines the position of the block in the intention list. The intention list consists of a sequence of *intention records*. The content of a record is shown in figure 6.3.

An intention record contains information that is pertinent to a disk block update, such as the address of the disk block (device no. and disk block no.), the extent of the update (offset and length). The disk block must not be modified before the transaction commits. Instead, the data of the update has to be stored in the intention list. Depending on the data size, the data can be stored as a part of the record. After a transaction commits, the data are written to the cached copy of the disk block in the NVRAM buffer.

Alternatively, the data can be stored in a "shadow" buffer block. After a transaction commits, any parts of the disk block which have not been over-written are copied to the shadow block and the "shadow" block is then switched atomically to become the definitive copy of the disk block. The purpose of having two ways of storing transaction data is to minimise data copying. Hence, the "shadow" block approach is used for updates which are larger than half of a disk block.

If a transaction only changes part of a disk block, the disk block must be cached in the NVRAM buffer before the transaction commits. The intention record contains the buffer block number which points to the cached copy. However, if the disk block is completely overwritten, there is no need to cache the disk block. In this case, the new image of the disk block is contained in the "shadow" disk block which will be switched to become the definitive copy after the transaction commits.

There are several types of intention records. The first type is for *byte-level updates*, i.e. for those updates that are multiples of a byte. For this type of update, the new data are simply written over the old data after a transaction commits. Other types of intention records are for *bit-level updates*, i.e. for those updates that can be as small as a single bit. These updates are performed on allocation bitmaps, i.e. the disk block and the byte segment header[1] allocation bitmaps. The data stored in the intention list are bit-masks. After a transaction commits, the bitwise AND/XOR function is performed on a bit-mask and the old data to produce the new data.

6.3.4 Committing Transactions

The state of a transaction is determined by a *commit bit*. This bit (C) is stored in the descriptor of the first buffer block (sequence no. 0) of the transaction's intention list (figure 6.3). The bit is set if and only if the transaction has committed. This is done with a single memory store instruction. A transaction commits with the following sequence of actions:

T1 A special record is written to indicate the end of the intention list.

T2 The *commit bit* is set. This is the commit point of the transaction.

T3 The intention list is processed.

T4 The *commit bit* is cleared.

T5 The buffer blocks of the intention list are released.

During the processing of the intention list, updates have to be made permanent. If the new data to be written to a disk block are recorded in an intention record, the data are simply written to the block buffer that caches the disk block. On the other hand, if the new data are recorded in a shadow block, the shadow block is switched to become the definitive copy of the disk block. This is done by changing the buffer block descriptors of the shadow and the original buffer blocks. After a buffer block is updated, it is queued for writing back to the disk. The disk write operations are processed asynchronously.

6.3.5 Recovery

When a system fails inadvertently and is restarted later, any internal inconsistency must be corrected before the system can enter normal service again. The recovery process consists of the following steps:

1. Determines the state of each NVRAM buffer block.

2. Notes all the intention lists that are active at the time of the crash.

3. Discards the intention lists which are not committed.

4. Completes the transactions from the committed intention lists.

5. Writes back all the cached disk blocks in the NVRAM buffer.

---

[1] This metadata structure will be explained later in the chapter

The state of each NVRAM buffer block is determined by reading the content of its descriptor. Also, the intention lists of the executing transactions at the time of the crash are reconstructed using the information recorded in the buffer block descriptors.

If the commit bit of an intention list is not set, the transaction has not reached **T2** (section 6.3.4) or it has already passed **T4**. In either case, the list can be safely discarded. If the commit bit is set, the transaction has completed **T2** but has not reached **T4**. In this case, the transaction is restarted at **T3**.

6.3.6   A Loose End

The discussion so far assumes that non-volatile RAM is as "safe" as disks. In other words, the chance of NVRAM corruption when a system fails is as unlikely (or likely) as disk corruption. There is no clear evidence to show that this is the case. On the contrary, Needham et al. [NHM86] point out that NVRAM could be more vulnerable than disks. A misbehaving CPU or a software bug could cause incorrect data to be written anywhere in the processor's address space. If NVRAM is handled like ordinary memory, it is vulnerable to corruption by these faults. In theory, a disk is also vulnerable to the same faults but it is far less likely in practice because the access hardware is more complex and the chance of setting up the hardware to write data to disk by accident is very remote. Needham et al. propose that a simple hardware enforced barrier (embedded in the micro-code of the processor) between the NVRAM and the CPU should greatly increase the robustness of the NVRAM against this kind of corruption.

Tim Wilson [Wil92b] performs some experiments on NVRAM protection using the protection facility provided by a processor's memory management unit. He tests the strength of the scheme by modifying the content of the processor's registers and some memory locations in order to simulate hardware/software faults. However, the result is not conclusive and does not show any apparent reduction in the corruption rate when the protection scheme is enabled.

With the advent of new microprocessors [Sit92] [KH92] that support 64-bit virtual address space, the sparseness of the address space may be sufficient to catch any "run-away" software errors. Other solutions [HCHJ91] [BBLP86] have been reported in the literature. This work does not investigate NVRAM protection. However, the design would still be valid with any NVRAM protection scheme as long as the NVRAM remains byte addressable.

6.4   Metadata

This section describes the organisation of the BSC's metadata on disk. The organisation is shown in figure 6.4.

Each byte segment is associated with a *byte segment header*. The header contains the byte segment's identifier, the size, the block address of the *primary extent directory* and the *minimum extent size*. The primary extent directory of a byte segment will be explained later. The *minimum extent size* defines how contiguous a byte segment is stored on disk. This is the smallest sequence of contiguous disk blocks that must be allocated as the byte segment is extended.

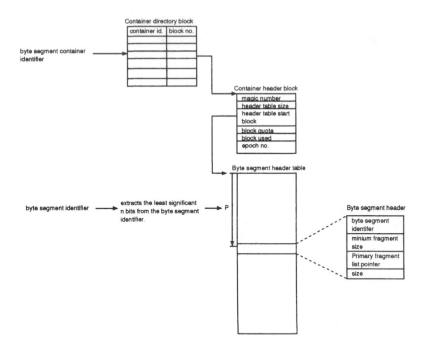

Figure 6.4: On-disk Metadata Structure.

Byte segment headers are grouped together in *byte segment header tables*. Each table is associated with one byte segment container. A container is described by a *container header block*. This block contains the address of the byte segment header table. It also contains: the *epoch number* which is used in generating byte segment identifiers; and the maximum and the current disk block usage of this container and its byte segments.

Each disk has a *container directory block*. This directory records all the byte segment containers that are stored on the disk. Each entry in the directory maps a byte segment container identifier to the address of the container header block. A container can be created dynamically. Disk blocks are allocated to store the new container header block and byte segment header table. The address of the container header block and the identifier is then entered into the container directory block.

During the start up phase of the BSC, the *container directory block*, which is stored at a fixed location on disk, is read. The *container header blocks*, which are pointed to by the directory entries, are then read from disk. The container directory blocks and the container header blocks are held in (volatile and non-volatile) memory during normal operations. On the other hand, the byte segment header tables are too large to cache entirely in memory and only some parts of the tables are cached at any time.

Generating Byte Segment Identifiers

In general, a byte segment identifier is an arbitrary bit-pattern and it is necessary to use a hashing function or B-tree structure to resolve an identifier to the address of a byte segment header. In this implementation, byte segment identifiers are generated in such a way that simple modulo arithmetic on an identifier would yield the position of the byte segment header in the header table. This simplifies the mapping of identifiers to byte segment headers considerably. The algorithm to generate new bit-patterns for object identifiers has been discussed in chapter 5. The following describes how the algorithm is implemented in the BSC.

The size T of the byte segment header table is equal to 2^n for some $n < 32$. The *epoch number* E is a 64 bit number. Initially, the number contains the container instance number (20 bits) in bits 43 to 63 and all other bits are zeros. Furthermore, the header entry index of the last created byte segment is stored in a counter M.

To create a new byte segment, an empty header entry in the byte segment header table is selected. The index of the chosen header is N. The objective is to generate a new bit-pattern, as the identifier for the byte segment, which contains N in the least significant n bits of the bit-pattern. This is done as follows:

Step 1 If $N \leq M$, set $E \leftarrow E + T$.

Step 2 Set $M \leftarrow N$.

Step 3 Set the new byte segment identifier $\leftarrow E + N$.

Notice that older byte segments that used the same header entry previously would have the same pattern in the least significant n bits of their identifiers. However, the identifier of the byte segment which presently occupies the header entry is stored in the entry as well and must be checked before any operation is performed.

The main problem in generating the bit-pattern is to ensure that bit-patterns are never reused. This is guaranteed, as has been explained in chapter 5, by the fact that E is never reset to a smaller value. One can increase E by the size of the table T every time a new bit-pattern is generated. In this way, every new bit-pattern, with the header entry index contained in the least significant n bits, is guaranteed to be unique. However, this is a rather inefficient use of the name space and, if the table size is large, would quickly exhaust the available name space.

Alternatively, if one can ensure that $E + N$ has never been issued, there is no need to advance E. The method described above is a simple way to ensure this. The basic idea is to guarantee that any values above $E + M$ have never been generated before. M stores the header entry index of the last created byte segment. If N is less than M, $E + N$ cannot be used because it may have been issued previously. In this case, E is increased by T. The new value of $E + N$ is greater than $E_{original} + M$ and the uniqueness guarantee is maintained. On the other hand, if N is greater than M, $E + N$ is greater than $E + M$ and can be used right away. The search for a free header entry has to be tuned so that N is usually larger than M (hence E does not have to be increased). This can be achieved quite simply by directing the search for a free entry to start from the entry indexed by M and to proceed towards the end of the header table. If a free entry is found before the search has to wrap around, N is greater than M.

M is kept in volatile memory and is initialised to 0 when the custode starts up. E is also kept in volatile memory. E is always smaller than the *epoch number* in the *container header block*. As E is increased to the same value as the header block value, a new value, $(E + T * X)$ for some number X, is written to the header block. This eliminates the need to update the header block value every time E is changed.

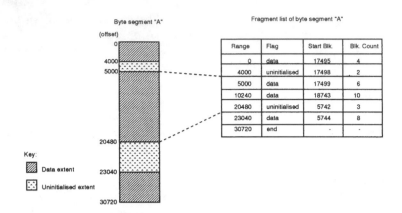

Figure 6.5: A Sample Byte Segment Extent List. A byte segment is shown diagrammatically on the left hand side. Uninitialised fragments are regions that have not been written to. The corresponding extent list is shown on the right. Notice that a data fragment (e.g. offset 5000-20480) can be split into more than one extent when the blocks allocated for the fragment are not contiguous. Also, if the boundary between a data fragment and an uninitialised fragment is not aligned on a disk block boundary (e.g. offset 4000), the uninitialised region up to the next block boundary is backed by the same disk block as the preceding data.

Finally, when byte segments are imported into a container, it is not possible to ensure that the least significant n bits of the byte segment identifiers contain the indices of the header entries. These "foreign" identifiers must be resolved by other means, such as by a B-tree structure. The resolution of "foreign" identifiers has not been implemented but it is believed that there will be no insurmountable difficulties in extending the present design to accommodate this need.

Extent Lists

In the following, the terms, *fragment* and *extent*, will be used frequently. A *fragment* is a logically continuous region in a byte segment. An *extent* is a *fragment* which occupies a sequence of contiguous disk blocks.

In the BSC disk space allocation is extent-based and the mapping from a byte segment offset to a disk block address is recorded in an *extent list*. An extent list consists of a number of extent entries, an example is shown in figure 6.5. The boundaries of an extent are defined by the range values of a consecutive pair of entries. Other fields in the first entry determine the extent type, which may be *data* or *uninitialised*, and the sequence of contiguous disk blocks allocated for the extent. Similarly, the second entry contains the information about the next extent. As illustrated in figure 6.5, a *data* fragment may be split into multiple extents if the disk blocks allocated to store the fragment are not contiguous. Also, an *uninitialised* fragment may not be in alignment with disk block boundaries. In this case, the *uninitialised* region up to the next block boundary is backed by the same disk block as the preceding data.

Given a byte segment offset, the extent that includes the offset can be determined by

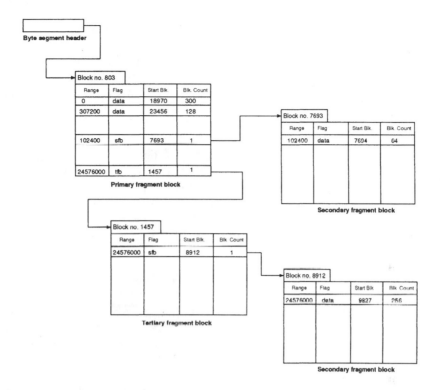

Figure 6.6: On-Disk Representation of an Extent List.

performing a binary search on the range values of the extent entries. The time to locate the target extent is in the order of $log_2 N$.

The number of entries in an extent list can vary and disk space must be allocated dynamically to store the extent list. New extents are added to the end of the list as the byte segment is extended. The extent entries for an *uninitialised* fragment, in the middle of a byte segment, are removed when the fragment is written over completely. On the other hand, if the *uninitialised* fragment is only partially written over, new extent entries have to be added to record the newly formed *data* fragment.

If a sequence of contiguous disk blocks is allocated to store an extent list, the whole list would have to be copied to a new disk sequence if the old one cannot be extended any further. Also, an insertion or deletion in the middle of a list would affect the rest of the list. These are practical problems for very long extent lists. Another alternative is to chain extent entries with pointers. Extent entries can be added or removed with no need to relocate other entries in the list. However, the entries have to be searched linearly by following the pointers in order to locate an extent that includes a byte segment offset. The searching time is in the order of N. This is very inefficient, especially for long extent lists.

Therefore, the BSC stores extent lists on disks as (unbalanced) tree structures that are expanded and contracted dynamically. The tree structure is shown in figure 6.6. When a byte segment is created, a disk block, called the *primary extent directory*, is allocated as the root of the tree. The address of this block is recorded in the byte segment header. A primary extent directory contains a number of extent entries. When these entries are filled up, new extent directories, which are called *secondary extent directories*, are allocated to store new extent entries. The addresses of these blocks are recorded in the primary extent directory. There is only a fixed number of slots in the primary extent directory to store address pointers to secondary extent directories. When these slots are exhausted, a tertiary extent directory is allocated. Additional secondary extent directories are allocated and their addresses are recorded in the tertiary extent directories.

The format of block address pointers in primary/tertiary extent directories is the same as extent entries (see figure 6.6). Moreover, the range value of the first extent entry in a secondary extent directory is recorded in the address pointer to the block. Similarly, the range value of the first block address pointer in a tertiary extent directory is recorded in the primary extent directory entry that contains the address pointer to the tertiary extent directory. With this arrangement, a binary search for an extent can be conducted recursively down the tree.

Notice that the number of blocks that have to be accessed in an extent search is one in the best case and three in the worst. The best case occurs when the extent is in the primary directory block, for instance, byte segment offset 307200 in the example shown in figure 6.6. The worst case occurs when the entry is in a secondary extent directory which is indirected through the tertiary extent directory, for instance, byte segment offset 24576000 in the example.

As extent directories are fixed in size, there is a problem when new entries have to be inserted into the middle of a fully populated secondary extent directories. Instead of shifting all the entries down the list to create an empty slot in the middle, which would be costly for a long list, a new extent directory is allocated to store a part of the original extent directory. The new entry is then inserted into the shortened block. The idea is illustrated in figure 6.7. In this way, the number of blocks affected by an insertion (or deletion) in the middle of an extent list is one in the best case and four in the worst. The best case occurs when the block is the last one in the list. The worst case occurs when the address pointer to the new secondary extent directory overflows into the tertiary extent directory.

In summary, the extent list representation presented in this section is chosen for three reasons. Firstly, disk space allocation is extent-based. Secondly, the unbalanced tree structure allows an extent list to grow to a very large size. This is important because the size of an extent list should not limit the size a byte segment can grow to. Finally, the format of extent directory entries is designed to allow fast searching through a long extent list. It also provides a compact way to record *uninitialised* fragments, irrespective of whether the fragments are in alignment with disk block boundaries.

It should be noted that for byte segments with only one extent, the allocation of the primary extent directory is not necessary because the location of the extent can simply be recorded in the byte segment header. Apart from the obvious advantage of saving disk space, this eliminates the need to perform an I/O operation for the extent directory. Hence, the translation from a byte segment offset to a disk address is faster and cheaper. At the moment, this has not been implemented but the design is ready to accommodate this optimisation.

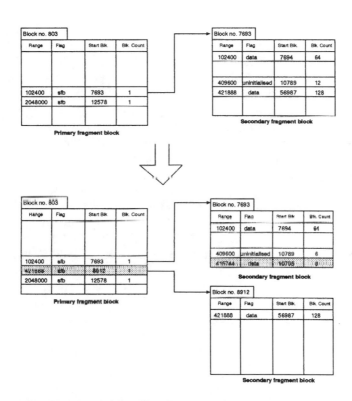

Figure 6.7: Inserting Entries in the Middle of an Extent List. This figure illustrates the necessary changes to an extent list when data are written to an *uninitialised* fragment. The fragment (409600-421888) shrinks to (409600-415744) and a new fragment (415744-421888) is formed. Part of the original secondary extent directory is copied to a new block and the new entry, shown shaded, is inserted into the original block. Notice that, after the change, the original block is no longer fully populated.

6.5   Disk Block Allocation

The BSC uses bitmaps to record the state of the disk blocks, i.e. whether they are allocated or free. The space required is very small. Only a single bit is needed to record whether a block is free. With 1 Kbytes block size, a 330 Mbytes disk only takes 42 Kbytes to store the bitmap. Therefore, all the disk block allocation bitmaps are locked in both volatile and non-volatile memory. It should be noted that updates to allocation bitmaps are co-ordinated by transactions. Hence, the on-disk image of a disk allocation bitmap, barring media failure, is always an accurate record of the state of every disk block.

Disk block allocation is extent-based. This method is chosen mainly because it supports fast sequential access with the allocation of disk space in (possibly) large units of physically adjacent disk blocks. This mode of access is important for continuous-medium data storage which the BSC is targeted to support. For each byte segment, the size of an extent must be larger than the *minimum extent size* stored in the byte segment header. This parameter is set to match the usage pattern of the byte segment. As will be explained in a later part of this dissertation, the parameter is set to a larger value to ensure that a byte segment, for storing continuous-medium data, can be accessed sequentially at a sustainable data rate.

The allocator uses the "first fit" approach to find a suitable extent for a byte segment. The search starts from the address of the last block of the byte segment. This improves the chance of allocating disk blocks contiguously for a byte segment. Also, a simple heuristic is applied to choose the size of an extent. At first, one unit, which is equal to the *minimum extent size*, is allocated to a byte segment; if it grows, two units are allocated; if it keeps growing, four units are allocated; and so on. This is a simple way to responds to byte segment extensions with the allocation of increasing portions of space.

External fragmentation is a problem with extent-based allocation because it affects the chance of finding the required number of contiguous blocks on disk. The general solution is to perform periodic reorganisation to gather small sequences of free space into bigger ones. Extent reorganisation has not been implemented but there should not be any difficulty in adding the facility in future.

In summary, the BSC uses a fairly conventional technique— extent-based allocation — to manage disk space. This technique has been used in numerous database and file systems. The main concern here is to have an allocation scheme which is suitable for fast sequential access.

6.6   Buffering and Disk I/O

It has been pointed out that the NVRAM buffer is divided into **fixed** size buffer units, called *buffer blocks*. In fact, a portion of the volatile memory is also divided into buffer block units. Unlike the NVRAM buffer blocks, which are used to cache disk blocks **and** store the intention records of NVRAM transactions, volatile buffer blocks are used solely for caching disk blocks.

There are two open hash tables: one for the NVRAM buffer blocks and the other for volatile buffer blocks (similar to the UNIX buffer cache). Buffer blocks which contain cache copies of disk blocks are linked together in the open hash tables and located by hashing the disk block numbers. A reference count is kept for each buffer block. A count of zero indicates that the block is not in use and can be reclaimed. These blocks are linked together in a free list but will remain in the hash tables until the blocks are finally reclaimed for other use. Also, buffer blocks which do not contain any valid data are linked together in an empty list.

Disk I/O operations are performed directly between the disks and the buffer blocks. These operations are performed asynchronously and a callback mechanism is provided to allow an arbitrary routine to be called when an I/O operation has completed.

All disk write operations are performed between the NVRAM buffer blocks and the disks. When a NVRAM transaction is completed, the NVRAM buffer blocks, which have been modified, are queued to be written back to disks. Because the execution of transactions and disk write operations are asynchronous, a transaction may modify a buffer block when a disk write operation is being executed to transfer data from the block to the disk. In this case, another disk write operation should be performed to flush the latest image of the disk block onto the disk. The state of a NVRAM buffer block is recorded in two bits— *dirty* and *I/O*. It can be in one of three states:

- *Dirty* is clear and *I/O* is clear. The buffer is not on the I/O queue and has not been modified since it was last written to disk.

- *Dirty* is clear and *I/O* is set. The buffer is on the I/O queue.

- *Dirty* is set and *I/O* is set. The buffer is on the I/O queue but the block has been modified since the block was queued.

There are two routines that can change the state of a NVRAM buffer block:

- *enqueue*. This routine queues a modified NVRAM buffer block for a disk write operation.

- *callback*. This routine is called when a disk write operation on the block has completed.

Table 6.1 shows how the routines change the state of NVRAM buffer blocks.

Initial State	Routine	
	enqueue	*callback*
dirty,I/O	*dirty,I/O*	*dirty,I/O*
clear,clear	clear,set	error
clear,set	set,set	clear,clear
set,clear	error	error
set,set	set,set	clear,set

Table 6.1: NVRAM Buffer Block I/O State Table.

The *enqueue* routine always examines the *I/O* bit before setting it. If the bit is clear, the buffer block is not on the I/O queue and it has to be queued. If the bit is set, the buffer block is already on the I/O queue. In this case, the routine just sets the *dirty* bit. When the *callback* routine is executed, it checks the status of the *dirty* bit. If the bit is not set, this indicates that the latest image of the disk block has been written by this disk write operation and the routine just clear the *I/O* bit and releases the buffer block. If the *dirty* bit is set, this indicates that a new disk write operation should be done to flush the latest image of the block to disk. In this case the *dirty* bit is cleared and the block is queued on the I/O queue again.

Buffer blocks in the I/O queues are sorted by their disk block numbers. CSCAN scheduling is used to select the disk blocks to perform the next I/O operation. Consecutive disk blocks are transferred in a single I/O operation. However, there is a limit to the maximum number of disk blocks per I/O operation. This is because the gather/scatter DMA table of the prototype hardware is limited to 128 entries and each buffer block occupies one entry. With 1 Kbytes block size, the maximum size of data that can be transferred in one I/O operation is 128 Kbytes.

Because buffer blocks are fixed in size, for large sequential I/O operations, long lists of buffer blocks have to be inserted into the I/O queues. Also the I/O queues become very long after a large burst of write traffic or when several large sequential I/O operations are initiated simultaneously. When the I/O queues were implemented as double linked lists and sorted by straight insertion, the performance deteriorates quickly as the length of an I/O queue increases. Hence, the I/O queues are implemented as *leftist trees* which is an efficient way to represent priority queues in the form of linked binary trees (due to C. A. Crane and detailed in [Knu73]). The insertion time is only of order $log_2 N$. The best case occurs when the tree is linear, and the worst case occurs when the tree is perfectly balanced. This property matches the insertion pattern of an I/O queue, especially when the I/O operations are highly sequential. Another advantage of the tree structure is that a long list of buffer blocks can be inserted into an I/O queue quickly and is independent of the length of the inserted list or the I/O queue.

As modified disk blocks are buffered in NVRAM, it is better to defer disk write operations to expedite disk read operations. This is a sensible optimisation because the latency incurred by a disk read operation would be reflected in the turnaround time of a byte segment operation whereas disk write and byte segment operations are completely asynchronous. Therefore, a simple selection policy is implemented. Disk read operations take precedence over disk write operations unless the number of modified blocks exceeds a high water mark.

6.7   Other Implementation Details

The prototype is implemented on a VME system. It has a 25MHz MC68030 processor and 8 Mbytes memory. The NVRAM buffer is made of 4 battery back-up memory cards. Each has 1 Mbytes static RAM on board. A special circuitry on the card monitors the 5V supply. If the power line voltage drops below 4.7V, it would isolate the card from the bus and switch to the battery supply. Secondary storage is provided by two 330 Mbytes SCSI-1 disks. The disks are connected to the host via an intelligent SCSI controller. The main processor handshakes with the controller via dual port RAM. Once a command is started, the main processor is relieved of any further action until the command is completed.

The prototype runs as a user-space process on top of the WANDA kernel [Dix91]. The kernel supports multiple pre-emptive threads per process. The IPC mechanism is designed to minimise the cost of data copying. A set of physically contiguous buffers are mapped into the user address space. Data are transferred between the network interface and the buffers directly. Arguments or results of a remote procedure call are marshalled directly into an IPC buffer.

The system runs in the "single address space" mode, i.e. with virtual memory management disabled. The disk driver is split into two halves, one half resides in the kernel and the other in the user space. The kernel driver is responsible for the execution of SCSI commands and the setting up of the gather/scatter DMA hardware. The user-space driver executes a disk I/O operation by sending SCSI commands to the kernel driver. It also constructs a DMA table from a list of buffer blocks. This table is passed to the kernel driver and data are transferred directly between the buffer blocks and the disks.

The prototype exports a remote procedure call (RPC) interface. The RPC system is called MSRPC. The system uses MSNL [McA90], which is a light weight virtual circuit protocol, as the transport. State associated with the binding between the client and server is maintained at the endpoints, and the virtual circuit identifier (VCI) of the network connection between them is the only identifier needed to uniquely specify a communicating tuple.

6.8 Summary

The chapter has presented the design of a byte segment custode. The byte segment custode offers good semantics in terms of failure recovery because all byte segment operations are executed atomically. A transaction facility is built around non-volatile memory to support the execution of byte segment operations atomically. Based on the design, a fully functional prototype has been implemented. The initial experience with the prototype is presented in the next chapter.

7

The Performance of the BSC

The BSC is designed to support atomic update semantics. The aim is to provide byte segments with clean update semantics so that the tasks to implement different file abstractions on top are greatly simplified. On the other hand, better semantics do not justify high performance costs. The use of NVRAM raises the possibility that atomic semantics can be provided at high performance. The BSC is a design to explore this possibility. Also, the prototype BSC is used in the prototype implementation of *rate-based* sessions, which will be described in chapter 9.

In this chapter, some preliminary measurements of the BSC performance are presented. This is followed by a discussion on the related work in the use of NVRAM in storage services.

7.1 Performance

7.1.1 Best-case Performance

Table 7.1 gives a sample of the best-case performance of the BSC. Section 6.7 describes the hardware and software characteristics of the prototype from which the measurements were taken. The table shows the cost to create a byte segment, to write 1 Kbytes to the byte segment, to read 1 Kbytes from the byte segment, to set the byte segment length to 512 bytes, to read the byte segment length and to delete the byte segment. These figures represent the best-case performance because the right data are all cached in (the volatile or non-volatile) memory and no I/O is necessary to perform the operations.

The figures help to highlight the performance advantage of using NVRAM. The NVRAM buffer serves as a buffer in the true sense of the word by decoupling the activity of the processor and the disk. For instance, each write operation in the test actually results in 4 disk blocks being written to. If these disk writes were to be performed synchronously, the performance would suffer badly. By using NVRAM, the time to perform the operation is only 1.5 ms, which can never be achieved if any synchronous disk write is required.

	Operations					
	create	write	read	setlength	getlength	delete
Operation Cost (ms)	1.4	1.5	0.9	1.2	0.1	1.3

Table 7.1: The Best-Case Performance of the BSC. The figures were obtained from an experiment to create 1000 byte segments, write 1 Kbytes to each of them, read 1 Kbytes from each of them, set the length of each byte segment to 512 bytes, get the length of each byte segment, and finally delete all the byte segments. The NVRAM buffer is big enough to cache all the disk blocks read or modified throughout the experiment. The figures shown are the time spent by the BSC to perform the operations.

7.1.2 Performance Cost of Atomic Writes

The following experiment was conducted to measure the cost of performing a byte segment write operation. The experiment consists of multiple runs. Each run consists of 10000 invocations of the write operation. In a run, all invocations repeat the same command, which is to write a fixed number of bytes to the same byte segment starting at offset 0. The length of the byte segment remains the same throughout the experiment. Each invocation simply overwrites existing data in the byte segment. Different runs write different number of bytes (in half Kbytes increment) per invocation. The timing measurements were obtained by reading a hardware counter at critical points in the BSC code. The counter is accurate to one μs but the software overhead to read the counter reduces the accuracy to 25 μs.

The time to execute each write operation can be broken down into three parts:

setup time the time spent to locate and obtain exclusive access to the in-memory metadata structure.

prepare time the time spent to process the update before the commit. This includes the time to copy data into the NVRAM buffer.

commit time the time spent to make the update permanent after the transaction commit point.

Figure 7.1 shows the time spent to perform the three phases of a write operation.

Setup time

As expected, the *setup time*, shown in figure 7.1a, is independent of the size of data written.

Prepare time

The *prepare time* is shown in figure 7.1b. In this phase, the BSC has to copy data from volatile memory into the NVRAM buffer. The *copy time* shown in the figure represents the time to copy the data. This copy action is unavoidable irrespective of the implementation techniques. So the difference between the *prepare time* and the *copy time* is the processing overhead. The processing overhead ranges from 163 μs for 1 byte to 865 μs for 7 Kbytes.

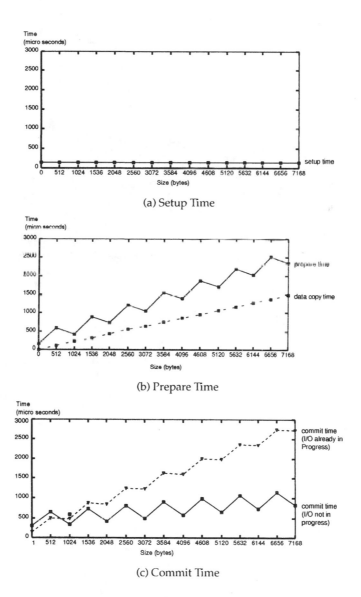

(a) Setup Time

(b) Prepare Time

(c) Commit Time

Figure 7.1: Cost Breakdown of Atomic Write. The time to execute each write operation can be broken down into three parts: the *setup time*, the *prepare time* and the *commit time*. These components are shown in the three graphs above.

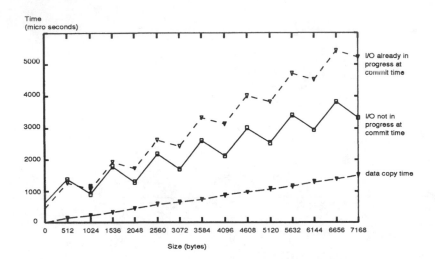

Figure 7.2: Cost of Atomic Write. The figure shows the upper and lower bound of the cost of atomic write. The time to perform the (unavoidable) data copy is also shown. If the write operation is not implemented as an atomic action, the processing time would still be larger than the data copy time.

It is more expensive to write half a block (512 bytes) than to write a complete block (1024 bytes). The data of a half block write are stored as part of the write's intention records and the data of a full block write are stored separately in a "shadow" buffer block. The higher processing overhead for half block writes indicates that the present implementation is not very efficient in dealing with intention records and has to be improved.

Commit time

The *commit time* is shown in figure 7.1c. For a given write size, the *commit time* varies between an upper and a lower bound. The two boundary values are shown in the figure. The lower bound corresponds to the case where none of the original block copies is on the I/O queue. The upper bound corresponds to the case where all of the original block copies are on the I/O queue. The two cases are handled differently. In the former case, "shadow" blocks are switched to replace the original blocks. In the latter case, buffer block switching is not possible without removing the block(s) from the I/O queue. Instead, the original blocks are overwritten by the new data.

While whole block writes can be made permanent by block switching, data of half block writes have to be copied (again) at commit time to the blocks that contain the original copies. This explains why the *commit* time for half block writes is higher than for whole block writes.

Total processing time

Figure 7.2 shows the overall cost of atomic writes, which is the sum of the *setup time, prepare time* and *commit time*. Also shown in the figure is the time to perform the unavoidable data copy from the volatile memory to the NVRAM buffer. It is not possible to pin down how much time could be saved if the write operation is not implemented as an atomic action. However, the processing time minus the data copy time, normally, is only 1.7 ms per 7 Kbytes. Any reduction in processing time by not having atomic semantics is not going to be significant. Moreover, the results are obtained from a prototype which has not been optimised; its performance can certainly be improved.

7.1.3 Recovery Time

The decision to keep the states of update operations entirely in the NVRAM buffer was found to be an important factor that greatly reduces the implementation complexity. There is no need to keep any redundant information on disk for recovery. As a rough indication of the implementation complexity, the source code to implement the NVRAM transaction facility is about 2000 lines of C while the BSC as a whole is written in 18000 lines of C. More importantly, the cached disk blocks can be written back to disk in any order. Hence, the scheduling of disk I/O operations can be optimised to improve I/O throughput.

The crash recovery process is very simple (section 6.3.5). Only the NVRAM buffer is scanned during crash recovery. There is no need to scan or repair any data structure on disk. In the prototype, it takes 287 ms to scan the 4 Mbyte NVRAM buffer during crash recovery. The custode can enter into service immediately after all the committed updates found during the scan have been made permanent.

7.1.4 I/O Throughput

The I/O throughput was measured when a 100 Mbyte byte segment was created (*create-sequential write*); when the byte segment was overwritten sequentially (*sequential overwrite*); and when the byte segment was overwritten randomly (*random overwrite*). The results are shown in figure 7.3. The figure is a plot of the I/O throughput against the NVRAM buffer size.

Sequential overwrite

The figure shows that the I/O throughput apparently increases with the NVRAM buffer size. In fact, the increase in the I/O throughput should be attributed to the merging of disk writes to consecutive blocks into large disk writes. Higher throughput is achieved with larger disk writes because delays, such as controller overheads and rotational latencies, are amortised over longer transfer times. The larger is the NVRAM buffer size, the larger is the number of disk blocks that can be merged into a single write and the higher the throughput is achieved.

The prototype has a limit on the I/O size (128 blocks). As the average size of disk writes approaches this value, the I/O throughput levels off. This is the reason why the I/O throughput levels off quickly after the NVRAM buffer size increases beyond 512 blocks. Even if there is no hardware restrictions on the I/O size, extremely large disk writes can

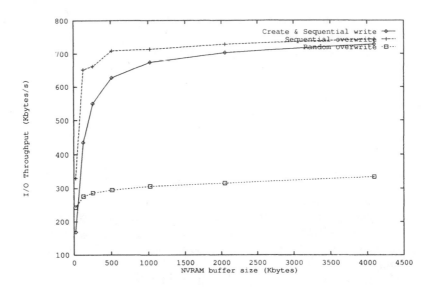

Figure 7.3: I/O throughput. The figure shows the I/O throughput to write a 100 Mbyte byte segment. Each write is 8 Kbytes in size.

cause potentially unacceptable delay to any (synchronous) disk reads that queue up be-hind them. Carson and Setia [CS92] analytically derive the optimal write size that min-imises read response time. They find that the value lies between 50 to 70 Kbytes and is primarily dependent on disk characteristics. (The derivation is presented in the context of a log-structured file system but it can be applied to any system which performs large writes.)

Create-sequential write

For the same NVRAM buffer size, the I/O throughput with *create-sequential write* is lower than *sequential overwrite*. The difference can be explained by the fact that *create-sequential write* involves metadata updates while *sequential overwrite* does not. Currently, metadata blocks, like ordinary data blocks, are queued for disk writes immediately after they are modified. The fairness property of the CSCAN disk scheduling algorithm ensures that these metadata writes would not be deferred indefinitely. Hence, large sequential data writes are interrupted by small metadata writes and this has the effect of lowering the I/O throughput.

An obvious optimisation which can improve the I/O throughput is to delay the writing of metadata blocks for a certain time. In this way, there will be fewer disk writes for meta-data blocks as multiple writes to the same block will be folded into a single disk write. The same argument can be applied to any disk block that is modified repeatedly. If these blocks can be identified, which requires more work with normal data, the I/O bandwidth can be better utilised by deferring the write-back of these blocks. Empirical data [RW93] from working systems show that a large number of disk writes are directed at a small number of blocks within a short duration. This observation suggests that delaying the write-back of only a small number of repeatedly accessed blocks can significantly reduce the number of disk writes. Further work is needed to assess the full benefit of this approach.

Random overwrite

With *random overwrite*, there is little chance that the disk blocks are modified consecutively. So disk writes can rarely be merged. However, the CSCAN disk scheduling algorithm re-orders disk writes so that the disk arm movement is minimised. The longer is the I/O queue, the shorter is the distance between two consecutive disk writes. A larger NVRAM buffer can accommodate a longer I/O queue, so the random I/O throughput should increase with the NVRAM buffer size.

The results show that the I/O throughput does improve with larger NVRAM buffer size. However, the increase is modest. The I/O throughput increases by 37% (from 243 Kbytes/s to 334 Kbytes/s) as the NVRAM buffer size increases by 170 times (from 24 Kbytes to 4 Mbytes). The increase in throughput is largely due to the reduction in disk seek time. Other sources of I/O delay, such as controller overheads and rotational latencies, are not reduced.

Since there is no constraint on the order in which cached disk blocks in the NVRAM buffer are written back to disk, there is the possibility that disk scheduling algorithms, such as CSCAN , could be more effective in improving the I/O throughput. The effect should be more prominent with a larger NVRAM buffer. The simple experiment presented above helps to illustrate that there is a performance limiting factor this high-level scheduling cannot surmount. The re-ordering of disk writes by the disk scheduling algorithm only reduces the seek time and improves the I/O throughput modestly. The scheduling algorithm does not (or cannot) take into account the rotational latency, which is another contributing factor to the I/O delay. It seems that a SATF scheduling algorithm that takes both seek and rotation position into account could do a better job (SATF stands for short-est access time first [JW91]). However, such an algorithm cannot be used in the high-level software because low-level device details, such as the position of the disk head, are simply not available. Perhaps in the long term, disks should be made more intelligent to handle the scheduling and even data organisation decisions, like the self organising disk proposed by [ES92]. Nowadays, capable microprocessors are cheap enough to be put to control disk drives. It will be interesting to see whether these devices can perform the data placement and scheduling functions better than the high-level software.

This section has presented some preliminary measurements of the BSC performance. The results show that the prototype performs reasonably well.

7.2   Related Work

This section presents an analysis of related work, concentrating on the use of NVRAM in the systems.

7.2.1   Existing systems

The use of NVRAM to improve disk performance is not new. IBM uses four megabytes of NVRAM on the 3990-3 disk controller [MH88]. Disk writes go to this non-volatile speed matching buffer to reduce latency. The buffered blocks are sorted in order to reduce the disk head movement in writing these blocks back to disk. Similarly, traditional distributed file systems, such as NFS, also use NVRAM to reduce disk traffic.

Sun NFS and Legato Prestoserve

Sun's Network File System (NFS) [SGK$^+$85] is currently the de facto standard distributed file system for workstations. The protocol specification [Sun89] is publicly available and is widely supported by vendors of UNIX machines. NFS servers are stateless, i.e. each operation is independent and must be completed before returning. This property implies that all disk writes performed in an operation must be synchronous.

Legato's Prestoserve [MSC$^+$90] is an add-on product to improve the write performance of NFS servers. It uses a NVRAM buffer to cache disk writes. The cached disk blocks are written out asynchronously. Prestoserve is designed to work with the BSD FFS [MJLF84] as the underlying file system. No change to the file system code or the on-disk data structures is required. The NVRAM cache is accessed via the *block device* interface, which is the same interface used by the file system to access the disk hardware.

In contrast with the BSC, Prestoserve represents a different approach to the use of NVRAM. The NVRAM buffer is **separated** from the file system in Prestoserve; whereas it is fully **integrated** in the BSC.

One advantage of putting the NVRAM buffer behind the device interface is that the file system would work regardless of whether the NVRAM buffer is installed. The difference is in the performance and not the behaviour of the system. This advantage is important especially when a NVRAM buffer is retrofitted to an existing file system.

Another advantage of the separation is that the device interface, if it is implemented in hardware, can protect the NVRAM buffer from "runaway" software errors (section 6.3.6).

However, the separation also means that the file system is not able to exploit the NVRAM buffer to offer better update semantics or faster recovery. The same recovery process has to be used regardless of whether the NVRAM buffer is installed. In the BSD file system, all directories and *inodes* (file metadata) have to be scanned to detect and repair any inconsistencies. The cost of these scans is already high (tens of minutes in typical configurations), and it is getting higher as storage systems expand. Other file systems [Hag87] [CAK$^+$92] [CMR$^+$90], which use logs to record metadata updates, can recover in a much shorter time. However, they are likely to be somewhat more complicated than the BSD file system. In contrast, the BSC only needs to scan the NVRAM buffer on recovery. The implementation is simple and the recovery process can be completed in a very short time (section 7.1.3).

7.2.2   Performance Studies

This work has not studied empirically the performance benefit of NVRAM caching with real workloads. However, other work [RW93] [BAD$^+$92] has used data collected on working systems to analyse the effect of NVRAM caching. Their results show that even a small NVRAM cache can bring about significant performance improvement.

Ruemmler and Wilkes [RW93] use trace-driven simulations to analyse the effect of write caching at the disk level. The traces were obtained from three systems over a two month period. The three systems studied are: a timesharing system, a file server and a personal workstation. The systems use a version of the BSD file system. They find that short bursts of writes are common and these writes go much faster even with just a small non-volatile cache at each disk. Furthermore, they observe a great deal of block overwriting: the same block would be written to disk over and over again. These overwritten blocks are typically metadata blocks. Their results show that adding even 8 Kbytes of NVRAM per disk could reduce disk traffic by 10-18%, and 90% of metadata write traffic can be absorbed with as little as 0.2 MBytes of NVRAM per disk. They also determine what percentage of writes could be absorbed for a given amount of NVRAM. In 30 second intervals, 95% absorption is reached at 700 Kbytes (workstation), 1 Mbytes (server) and 4 Mbytes (time-sharing system).

Baker et al. [BAD+92] study the use of NVRAM as file caches on client workstations and on file servers. They use traces obtained from a Sprite distributed file system to drive their simulations.

Their measurements show that a one half megabyte NVRAM buffer on the server would reduce the number of disk writes for most file systems measured by about 20% and by 90% on one heavily used file system. Notice that the file systems measured are log-structured file systems (LFS) [RO91]. The file server has already been optimised to perform fewer disk writes than traditional file servers (at the expense of being less reliable). LFS batches together many small writes and transfers them to disk in one operation. In order to maintain large free extents for writing new data, LFS divides the disk into large fixed-size extents, called segments. Any given segment is always written sequentially from its beginning to its end. File data written into the server cache are accumulated there for up to 30 seconds. (This has the undesirable effect of introducing non-predictability into the semantics of writes.) The file data may also be flushed from the cache by *fsync* calls. The reported reduction in disk writes is due to the elimination of the disk writes caused by the 30 second limit or the *fsync* calls.

With a megabyte of NVRAM on diskless clients, their results show that the amount of file data written to the server is reduced by 40% to 50%. As in the case of the file server, data written to a client cache are written from the cache after about 30 seconds. Applications can also force file data from the client caches to the file server's disks immediately and synchronously using *fsync* calls. They find that most of the write traffic is caused by the 30 second limit or *fsync* calls and is not due to insufficient cache size.

7.2.3   LLSS

LLSS [Wil92b] is a research prototype designed by Tim Wilson, as part of his Phd research to increase the performance of network storage services (see also section 3.9.2). Like the BSC, the design has an integrated NVRAM buffer. However, LLSS uses the NVRAM buffer simply as a write-back cache. Modified disk blocks are written to the cache and then are written out to disk asynchronously. Although single blocks are updated atomically, multiple block extents are not. Therefore, the use of NVRAM in LLSS is, functionally, very similar to Prestoserve (described above).

7.3 Summary

The measurements presented in this chapter show that the BSC is able to support atomic update semantics without sacrificing performance. NVRAM has been used in existing file systems to improve write performance. However, the systems do not exploit the fast byte-level update characteristic of NVRAM to provide better update semantics. This work has not studied empirically the performance benefit of NVRAM caching with real workload. However, other work on this subject has provided encouraging evidence that even a small NVRAM cache can bring about a significant performance improvement.

8

Rate-Based Sessions: Concept & Interface

8.1 Introduction

In this chapter, the storage of continuous-medium data is considered. Early work in this area [Cal87] [TS87] only deals with voice storage. The bandwidth requirement of this medium type is low. Recent work [RV91] [AOG92] [GC92] [LS93] that deals with high bandwidth media, such as video, concentrates mainly on the hard real-time scheduling of disk transfers. Little attention has been given to the issue of system integration. Working systems [Hop90] or prototypes [Jar92] are mostly designed to serve in a specific environment and lack the flexibility to offer a general purpose service.

In contrast, this work looks at the storage issue from a different angle. The goal is to design a general purpose file service that can be used to store continuous-medium data encoded in a variety of formats. The service is to integrate with other services that support other file types. Moreover, the extra effort needed to support a new format should be minimal. These requirements call for a careful separation of storage functions into manageable components. These components can then be modified or evolved quite independently. Section 8.2 identifies the main components and the division of responsibilities among them.

Like other file types, continuous-medium files are stored as byte segments. The interface to access these byte segments must meet the temporal requirements of this file type. Section 3.8 has outlined the approach taken in this work, i.e. byte segment operations are grouped into sessions and each session is associated with a performance guarantee that matches the temporal requirements of continuous-medium data. These sessions are called *rate-based* sessions. The concept is discussed in section 8.3. The interface is explained in section 8.4 and section 8.5.

Basic operations
cf_create [fileCap, containerId, fileAttr] → [status, fileID]
cf_delete [fileCap, containerId, fileId] → [status]
cf_read [fileCap, containerId, fileID, offset, length] → [status, data]
cf_write [fileCap, containerId, fileID, offset, length, data] → [status]
High level operations
cf_dup [fileCap, containerID, fileID] → [status, newFileID] Duplicates a file.
cf_cut [fileCap, containerID, fileID, offset, length] → [status] Removes a file fragment.
cf_concat [containerID, fileCap1, fileID1, fileCap2, fileID2] → [status] Concatenates a file (fileID2) to the end of another file (fileID1).
Real-time delivery operations
cf_open [fileCap, containerID, fileID, translator, translatorParam] → [status, sessionID, sessionCap] Establishes a session with the translator.
cf_close [fileCap, sessionID] → [status] Closes the session.

Figure 8.1: The CFC interface.

8.2   The CFC and the Translator

The support of continuous-medium data depends on the close cooperation of three components. They are: the CFC, the *translator* and the BSC. The design of a BSC has been explored in chapter 6. This section outlines the functions of the CFC and the translator.

8.2.1   The CFC

The CFC provides a **generic** file service for continuous-medium data. It is a generic service because it treats each continuous-medium file as an uninterpreted stream of bytes. The flat file custode (FFC) also treats files as byte streams. However, the CFC provides additional functions that the FFC does not:

- The CFC provides a number of high level operations to facilitate the editing of these files. This is necessary because continuous-medium files are too voluminous to be edited by copying in the client domains (section 2.4).

- The CFC coordinates with the translator to deliver continuous-medium files for real-time presentations.

Of course, there are other differences as well, such as data caching policy. For the present discussion, it is not necessary to compare the two services in detail except to note that the CFC and the FFC are offering two distinct file abstractions and should not be mixed up.

Figure 8.1 shows the interface of the CFC. When a continuous-medium file is freshly recorded, it is represented internally as a single byte segment. File editing, such as cut and paste, may create new continuous-medium files out of old ones. These new files may be the concatenations of different fragments from different byte segments. So in general, each continuous-medium file is a list of fragments from different byte segments. Different files may share the same byte segment. It is the job of the CFC to detect and remove byte segments that are no longer referenced by any continuous-medium file.

The CFC does not handle the real-time delivery of continuous-medium files. It sets up a session with the translator and delegates the responsibility to the translator. To deliver a continuous-medium file in real-time is to send the file data as a stream of temporally spaced data samples. To do so requires the understanding of the stream specifics, including its encoding and timing information. If the real-time delivery function is not separated from the CFC, the CFC would have to be aware of the numerous encoding formats (section 2.4).

Of course, shifting the real-time delivery function to the translator does not remove the need to add format dependent code into the storage service, the translator is as much a part of the service as the CFC. However, this separation encourages modular designs. New translators can be built to accommodate new formats or to supersede old ones. Like a device driver, translators may be loaded dynamically to provide customised functions. If the problems with protection and security can be solved, users may even be able to download their own translators. This opens up new possibilities to extend the functions of the storage service.

The idea of customising a generic storage service with translators has its precedent Roger Calnan [Cal87] implements a voice storage service over a general purpose filing system. He also calls this voice service a *translator* and proposes that a video translator could be built for storing video data. However, video requires much higher bandwidth than audio, he has not explored how a video translator can ensure that the general purpose filing system can provide the necessary bandwidth. This is the question that this chapter attempts to answer.

8.2.2 The Translator

There will be different translators, where each translator handles a specific encoding format. Figure 8.2 illustrates the roles of the CFC, the translators and the BSC in managing streams with different encoding formats.

To establish a play-back session, the application issues a cf_open call to the CFC. An argument of this call is the name of the translator that is going to handle this session. Therefore, the binding between a file and a translator is dynamic[1]. For instance, a file may be converted into a different format by non-real-time processing, a different translator has to be specified to play back the file. The CFC passes on the request to the translator, together with a list of byte segments that have to be read during the session. This list corresponds to the internal representation of the file. The translator sets up a *rate-based* session with the BSC (see below) and returns a sessionID to the CFC for future reference. The translator also has to generate a capability (chapter 4) for the client so that it can interact with the translator directly. The sessionID and the capability are returned to the application.

The application can then start the play-back by calling the translator directly[2]. During the play back, the translator reads data from the byte segments and sends the data down

---

[1]It is up to the application to specify the correct translator, the CFC has no means to check this.

[2]Assume that the application has successfully connected the translator with the output device.

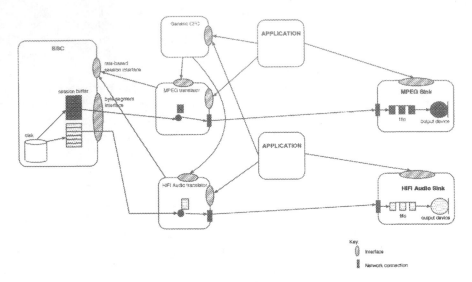

Figure 8.2: Handling Stream Heterogeneity.

the stream connection.

Both the translator and the BSC are on the critical path of the real-time data delivery. It is essential to minimise the delay and jitter that could be introduced by such interactions. For this reason, the translator and the BSC have to run on the same machine, and even in the same address space.

Mutually Synchronised Streams

The translator handles each playback session individually. As far as the translator is concerned, there is no temporal relation between concurrent sessions. In practice, there is a need to synchronise multiple streams. A common example is "lip-synching" between a video and an audio stream. This work assumes that multi-stream synchronisation is done by some agent outside the storage service. This agent can be a synchronisation service, such as the one described in [Sre92]. Sreenan proposes that synchronisation is better performed at the presentation node or close to it. This approach ensures better synchronisation because local delay and jitter can be determined and controlled more accurately. It might be beneficial to reduce the skew between two synchronised streams by coordinating their starting time. For this purpose, a group operation [Jar92] could be added to the translator to start multiple streams simultaneously.

The above discussion has established the context in which *rate-based* sessions are used. In the following, the concepts and the interface of these sessions will be discussed.

8.3 Resource Reservation and Scheduling

This section looks at the role of *rate-based* sessions as a vehicle to allow a BSC to reserve and schedule resources in order to support the presentation of continuous-medium streams.

8.3.1 The Need to Reserve Resources

The previous section established the function of a translator, which is to provide the timing control for data sample delivery (or acceptance). Typically, the translator reads some data from a BSC; sends the data down the stream connection; pauses for some time until it is time to deliver another sample; and repeats the previous sequence again.

How can the translator ensure that data samples are delivered in time? Assume there is no prior arrangement with the BSC. Reading data from the byte segments could be delayed by I/O operations. By the time the BSC returns the data, it may well have passed the delivery deadline for that data sample. The translator may buffer data internally and perform byte segment reads well in advance. The internal buffer can decouple the delivery of data samples from any delay caused by the byte segment reads. However, two questions need to be answered. What is the most suitable size for the internal buffer? How far ahead should byte segment reads be performed? Clearly, these parameters depend ultimately on the worst case delay a byte segment read could incur. However, this delay is beyond the control of the translator. Moreover, any buffering is useless if the BSC cannot sustain the data rate of the stream.

There is an implicit assumption in the argument just presented. The assumption is that, in the short to medium term, resources, such as buffer space and disk bandwidth, are limited relative to the demand of continuous-medium data. The contentions for limited resources inevitably introduce delay. There would be situations in which the demand for resources would exceed their capacities. Perhaps in the long term, technological advances would increase the resource capacities well beyond the demand of continuous-medium data. Resource contention and overload will rarely occur. Until then, these are practical concerns and call for two special measures:

- Resources should be reserved in advance of usage. A reservation request should be turned down when the expected demand is going to exceed the resource capacity.

- Resource utilisations should be carefully scheduled to meet the temporal requirements of continuous-medium data.

The arguments for resource reservation and resource scheduling can be applied to any component that is part of a system to support continuous-medium data. The term Quality of Service (QOS) is often used in the literature, especially in the context of computer networks, to describe application requirements. The negotiation between client and server for an acceptable QOS is a vehicle to establish the resource requirements and to reserve the resources in order to satisfy the requirements. The agreed QOS may even be a dynamic quantity and vary with the current state of resource utilisation. For instance, the QOS may degrade when the resources are over-utilised.

Coming back to the translator. There are different resources it has to utilise, such as the CPU cycles, the network bandwidth and the service provided by the BSC. These resources have to be reserved and scheduled in their own ways. In the following, the discussion will concentrate on how the BSC's resources can be reserved and scheduled, to satisfy the requirements of the translator. The wider issue of QOS provision in a system is beyond the scope of this work.

8.3.2 Rate-based Sessions

The translator establishes its requirements with the BSC through *rate-based* sessions. *Rate-based* sessions enable the BSC to foresee how byte segments are accessed. The BSC can buffer the data internally and perform read-ahead actions to decouple the I/O delay from byte segment reads. Byte segment writes can be handled in a similar way, data can be buffered in preallocated space and transferred back to disk at a later time. In fact, the allocation of buffer space can be done on a per-session basis. Having a dedicated **session buffer** for each session is advantageous because this eliminates a source of contention which can introduce undesirable delay.

As far as the translator is concerned, the BSC offers a better quality of service because the former no longer has to take into account any delay in byte segment reads caused by I/O operations. As for the BSC, it is given more information to enable it to reserve resources, such as buffer space and disk bandwidth, and to schedule their utilisations to meet the demand. The session set-up process allows the BSC to turn down any requests that cannot be met with the resources available.

8.3.3 The Difficulties in Resource Reservation

In order to reserve resources, the required capacities have to be determined. The question is how accurately the requirements can be foreseen.

Variable rate videos are bursty in nature, the instantaneous data rate can vary significantly from the average rate. Moreover, while the workloads of continuous-medium data are foreseeable, the same cannot be said for ordinary data, such as text and binaries. The workloads of these data are bursty and irregular. It is difficult to describe these workloads in any accurate way.

It is possible to make a reservation based on the maximum demand. For a variable-rate stream, resources can be reserved to cope with the maximum data rate. This way of making reservations has the advantage of being able to meet the demands from established sessions at all time. However, it is quite possible that different streams may not reach their peak demands simultaneously. The average utilisation of a resource may be much lower than the aggregate maximum. In other words, making worst-case reservations may lead to under-utilisation of resources. This has the undesirable effect of causing new sessions to be turned down unnecessarily.

If the probability of different sessions reaching their peak demands is low, more reservation requests can be granted. This has the positive effect of better resource utilisations and less rejections of reservation requests. On the other hand, temporary overload can occur, though with a very low frequency. Under these situations, a small fraction of data in a continuous-medium stream would be lost. However, such data losses may well be tolerated by the users. For instance, the loss of a few frames in a video stream may look like temporary interference that is familiar to television viewers.

It is still an open question whether the statistical multiplexing of different sessions with varying resource requirements can indeed be exploited to achieve better resource utilisations. However, the premise that continuous-medium data are resilient to occasional data loss is generally recognised. Hence, the "pessimistic" strategy of making worst-case reservations may well be an over-kill for continuous-medium data.

8.3.4 The Semantics of Rate-based Sessions

If the BSC does not make worst-case reservations, both the BSC and the translator have to prepare for the situations when temporary overload occurs. Under these circumstances, the BSC may not be able to transfer data from disk in time. If the translator tries to read the data, what is the appropriate response of the BSC? There are two possible answers. Firstly, the BSC can defer the reply until the necessary disk transfer is completed. Secondly, the BSC can reply immediately and inform the translator of the overload situation. It is then up to the translator to decide how to handle the situation.

The first approach is not attractive because it aggravates the effect of the overload condition. It is useless to return data to the translator that have passed their delivery deadlines. The disk bandwidth is wasted to transfer these data from disk. In order to catch up with the progress of the session, the BSC may well have to skip reading some data fragments entirely.

Therefore, the second approach is chosen in this work. This makes the semantics of byte segment accesses within a rate-based session slightly different from non-session accesses. Session reads would return no data if the BSC fails to read-ahead in time to transfer the data from the disk to its session buffer; non-session reads always return the required data. Similarly, session writes would be rejected if, as a result of the overload condition, its session buffer has been filled up with write-back data.

Having explained what a *rate-based* session is for and the semantics of byte segment accesses within *rate-based* sessions, the rest of this chapter will look at how the concept can be realised.

8.4 Rate-Based Sliding Window

The discussion in the previous section assumed that the BSC is able to foresee how byte segments are accessed. This enables the custode to perform read-ahead or write-behind to keep up with the session's progress.

However, one must be careful about how the information on future accesses is passed to the BSC. In particular, the BSC should not be burdened with the detailed timing of data sample delivery (or acceptance). Nor should the performance guarantee of *rate-based* sessions depend on the BSC interpreting the content of byte segments. The approach adopted in this work is described below.

The translator passes the information on future accesses to the BSC through the *rate-based* session interface (which is orthogonal to the byte segment interface). The interface will be described later. Before that, one has to understand the **sliding window** concept, which provides the basis for describing the progress of sessions.

8.4.1 Definition

The *sliding window* of a session can be viewed as an overlay on the byte segment. Projecting the window on the byte segment yields a fragment. This fragment is called the *scope* of the session at that moment. For a read session, the BSC makes sure that this fragment is cached in the session buffer. For a write session, the BSC pre-allocates space in the session buffer to store this fragment.

Conceptually, the window moves along the byte segment in increasing offset values[3] at a certain rate. The BSC reads ahead and makes sure that, at any moment, the *scope* of the session is cached in the session buffer. Similarly, at any moment, the BSC preallocates buffer space to store the *scope* of the session, and writes back the written data at a later time.

The behaviour of the *sliding window* can be described by two time-related functions, called the upper bound function $UBF(t)$ and the lower bound function $LBF(t)$ respectively. More precisely, the difference of the functions $UBF(t) - LBF(t)$ defines the *scope* of the session at the time t (see also figure 8.3).

The functions are defined in terms of the following parameters:

Session window size (S) It will become clear that the size of the *sliding window* can vary. This parameter defines the maximum size of the window.

Session peak rate (R) This is the rate at which the window moves (conceptually) along the byte segment.

Reference offset (X_0) This is a reference byte segment offset.

Reference time (T_0) This is a reference time.

With these parameters, the two functions are defined as follows:

$$
\begin{aligned}
UBF(t) &= R(t - T_0) + X_0 \\
LBF(t) &= \begin{cases} X_0 & \text{if } T_0 \le t \le (T_0 + S/R) \\ UBF(t) - S & \text{otherwise} \end{cases}
\end{aligned}
$$

Basically, the functions describe the following behaviour. At time T_0, the *sliding window* is at offset X_0 and is 0 in size. The session buffer is empty. Since then, the BSC starts filling the session buffer with data at rate R. When the data in the buffer reaches the full size of the window S (at time $T_0 + S/R$), the BSC starts removing data from the buffer at rate R as well. Thereafter, the amount of data kept in the buffer stays constant at S. Of course, this is only an interpretation. The BSC does not actually fill or empty data continuously. A more accurate picture of the BSC behaviour is shown in figure 8.3.

8.4.2 Relation with read-ahead scheduling

Sliding window provides a prediction model with which the BSC is able to make decisions on how and when to perform read-ahead and write-behind actions. The relation between sliding window and read-ahead scheduling is illustrated in figure 8.3.

---

[3]Or decreasing offset values if the stream is played backward instead of forward

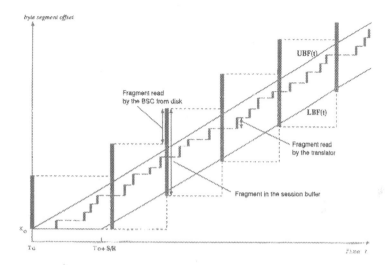

Figure 8.3: Sliding Window & Read-Ahead Scheduling. The figure is an $x - y$ plot with *time* on the x-axis and *byte segment offset* on the y-axis.

At any time t, $UBF(t) - LBF(t)$ defines the *sliding window* of the session. The *sliding window* is zero in size at time T_0 and increases to the maximum S at time $T_0 + S/R$. Its size remains constant afterwards.

At some time t, a *fragment* is transferred from the disk. A fragment is a logically continuous region in a byte segment. This event is marked by a vertical black strip at $x = t$. The projection of the strip onto the y-axis represents the position of the fragment in the byte segment. The fragment in the buffer after a disk transfer (at $x = t$) is the aggregate of the newly read fragment and the fragment already in the buffer, which is represented by a grey strip (at $x = t$) in the figure. The amount of buffer space allocated to the byte segment can be constant or varying. However, it must be bound because one cannot assume an unlimited supply of buffer.

The BSC must read in a fragment from disk before the fragment falls into the *sliding window*. If the BSC is overloaded, it may skip some fragment to catch up with the *sliding window*

A stepwise curve in the figure represents the byte segment accesses performed by the translator. Each step of the curve represents a fragment read by a byte segment read operation. The accesses are in step with the window progress, i.e. the fragment read by an access at time t falls within $LBF(t)$ and $UBF(t)$.

Write-behind (not shown in the figure) is similar to read-ahead. The BSC has to allocate buffer space for a fragment before it falls into the *sliding window*. Also, the BSC can write a fragment back to disk and reclaim the buffer space only when the *sliding window* has passed the fragment.

8.4.3   Relation with byte segment accesses

It is worth emphasising that byte segment accesses are orthogonal to the progress of the *sliding window*. A read access is granted if and only if the data requested are cached in the session buffer (section 8.3.4). Otherwise, the access is rejected. Similarly, a write access is granted if and only if buffer space has been pre-allocated for the data.

However, there is an indirect relation between byte segment accesses and the *sliding window*. The BSC uses the *sliding window* model to schedule read-ahead or write-behind actions. Hence, the data cached in the session buffer reflect the **predicted** session progress. The byte segment accesses, on the other hand, are directed by the translator and are performed in accordance to the **actual** session progress. Obviously, the two must match or else the prediction is of no value.

8.4.4   Variable rate sessions

In the absence of any intervention, the *sliding window* "moves" along the byte segment at a constant rate R. This model is adequate for fixed-rate sessions. For a variable-rate session, the actual progress of the session and the *sliding window* may diverge. The BSC would then fail to perform read-ahead or write-behind correctly.

This work takes the view that the translator is responsible for keeping the *sliding window* in synchrony with the progress of a session. A number of operations are provided at the *rate-based* session interface which can be used by the translator to adjust the *sliding window* of the session. These operations will be explained in section 8.5.2. The reasons for placing the burden on the translator are:

- The translator is responsible for the timing control of data delivery. Hence, it has all the information to perform the adjustments. On the other hand, the BSC is unaware of the detailed format or timing of data, it can only determine the actual progress of the session by observing the byte segment access pattern. This, in effect, is a process to reconstruct the timing information the translator already knows and is responsible for. This duplication of effort is not desirable.

- With the timing information, the translator is in a better position to foresee the timing of future accesses. For instance, information on medium term data rates may be embedded in a variable rate video stream, this information would allow the translator to estimate the medium term data rate of the session more accurately.

8.5   Rate-Based Session Interface

The session interface is divided into two parts:

- the set-up and shut-down of sessions, and

- the dynamic adjustment of *sliding windows*.

8.5.1 Session Set-up and Shut-down

Set-up

The translator establishes a *rate-based* session by invoking the open_session operation.

open_session [containerID, byteSegmentID, ticketAttribute] → [ticketID]

This is the standard way to establish any sessions (section 3.8.2), not just *rate-based* ones. The argument ticketAttribute contains a number of parameters:

- mode
- start
- length
- session peak rate
- session window size
- maximum rate

Mode specifies whether this is a read or write session. Start and length define the coverage of the session within the byte segment. If this is a write session, the coverage can extend beyond the current size of the byte segment. Session peak rate and session window size are parameters that define $UBF(t)$ and $LBF(t)$ of the session (section 8.4).

If this is a write session and the byte segment has not been written before, maximum rate defines the maximum rate at which the byte segment will be read in its lifetime. Otherwise, this parameter is ignored. The parameter helps the BSC to decide how to store the byte segment on disk to cater for a higher playback rate in the future. Notice that session peak rate and maximum rate can be different. For instance, session peak rate is set to the normal playback rate while maximum rate is set to the fast-forward rate.

A *rate-based* session can cover more than one byte segments. To set up such a session, open_group_session (section 3.8.2) is used. The operation is the same as open_session except that a list of tickets and one for each byte segment is returned. For rate-control purposes, the byte segments are required to be accessed consecutively in the same order as they are presented in the open_group_session argument.

An open_session request may be turned down by the BSC if it does not have sufficient spare resources to support the session. Also, each session only supports one stream. If multiple streams are to be presented in synchrony, multiple sessions have to be set up before the presentation can be started. It may be possible that some sessions in the group are turned down by the BSC. In that case, the application has to abort the presentation and retry at a later time.

After a session is set up, it is in a quiescent state and has to be "started" with a set_window operation. A session cannot remain in the quiescent state indefinitely, a time-out is associated with the session in this state. If this period is exceeded, the session is revoked unilaterally by the BSC. This time-out mechanism allows the BSC to recover any resources that are tied to sessions which are never started. Normally, this mechanism is not necessary because the translator can decide when to shut down a session. Nevertheless, this mechanism is useful to protect the BSC against translator misbehaviour or partial failures of the system in which the translator fails but the BSC continues to function.

After the session is started, the translator can access the byte segment(s) using write_bs or read_bs. The ticketID identifies to which session the access belongs (section 3.8.2).

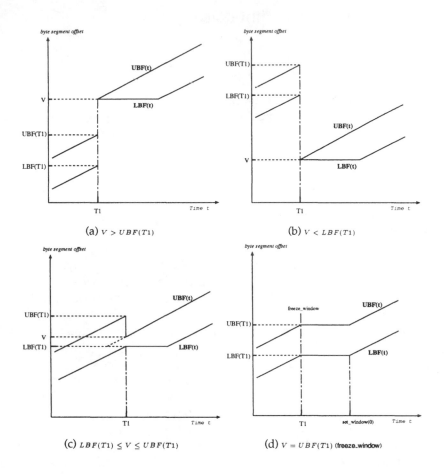

Figure 8.4: Sliding Window Adjustment. In each diagram, V is the new value of $UBF(t)$ after an adjustment, which happens at time $T1$. Notice that the window size may change as a result of the adjustment.

Shut-down

Once a session is started, it will end by default when the *sliding window* has gone beyond the coverage of the session. Alternatively, the translator can end a session prematurely by invoking the close_session operation (section 3.8.2). Like open_session, this is also a standard session operation.

8.5.2 Dynamic Window Adjustments

Normally a *sliding window* "moves" at a constant rate. However, the translator can adjust the position of the window when necessary using the following operations:

set_window [ticketID, offset] → [timeStamp]

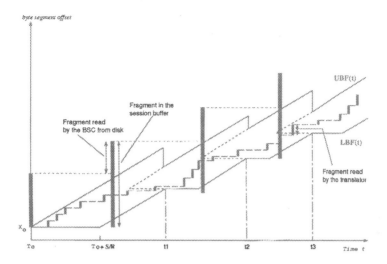

Figure 8.5: Variable-rate Session and BSC Read-Ahead. At time t1,t2 and t3, the window is adjusted downward to keep it in synchrony with the stream progress.

> Changes the value of $UBF(t)$. The net effect is to establish a new reference position for $UBF'(t)$ such that UBF(timeStamp) =offset.

adjust_window [ticketID, displacement] → [timeStamp]

> This operation has the same effect as set_window. The only difference is that set_window takes an absolute position (an offset into the byte segment) as an argument and this operation takes a relative displacement from the current position as an argument.

freeze_window [ticketID] → [timeStamp]

> This operation stops the window's progress. Window progress can be resumed with an adjust_window operation (displacement = 0).

The semantics of the operations are best explained diagrammatically, as it is done in figure 8.4.

When the new position of $UBF(t)$ immediately after a window adjustment is not within the *scope* of the window before the operation (figure 8.4a and 8.4b), there is no guarantee that the session buffer would contain the right data. For this reason the session should be considered as starting afresh with an empty session buffer and a reset *sliding window*. Seeking to a new index position during a video playback is an example of when this kind of window adjustment is useful.

Window adjustment operations can also be used to keep the *sliding window* in synchrony with the actual progress (figure 8.4c). When the window is moving too far ahead, an *adjust_window* call can move the window back to the position close to the actual progress. Figure 8.5 illustrates the use of adjustments to keep the *sliding window* in synchrony in a variable-rate session.

Despite the fact that window adjustments are light-weight operations, these adjustments constitute extra interactions between the translator and the BSC. If window adjustments are done frequently, this overhead could accumulate into a considerable CPU workload. Therefore, frequent window adjustments are not desirable.

If the data rate of a stream varies in a small range, this variation can be absorbed by an adequately sized sliding window. In that case, there is no need to adjust the window, even though the stream is variable-rate. In fact, some digital video standards are designed to minimise the data rate variations[4].

In general, the data rate of streams can vary over a large range. When the session rate (determined by the parameter session peak rate) and the instantaneous rate of the stream differ significantly, window adjustments have to be done frequently. This is not desirable.

Instead of requiring the translator to perform "down-calls" to the BSC, the BSC can be arranged to perform "up-calls" to the translator to find out the session's progress. This mode of interaction can cut down the need to perform window adjustments significantly. This is because the BSC only needs to determine the session progress when it is about to perform a disk transfer for the session. Between two consecutive disk transfers, there is no negative effect if the sliding window is not synchronised with the session progress. Therefore, window adjustments in this interval are saved with BSC up-calls. However, BSC up-calls should not be the default behaviour because, for streams with fixed data rates or small data rate variations, these up-calls are completely redundant.

Finally, if the translator can anticipate the medium term data rate of the stream, it can reduce the discrepancy between the session rate and the stream rate by adjusting the session rate accordingly. This helps to cut down the frequency of window adjustments.

8.6 Summary

The CFC provides a generic service for continuous-medium data. It treats each continuous-medium file as an uninterpreted stream of bytes. The real-time delivery of continuous-medium files are handled by translators. Each translator handles a specific encoding format.

To support the real-time delivery of continuous-medium data, resources have to be reserved in advance and their utilisations have to be scheduled carefully. *Rate-based* sessions provide the mechanism to allow the translator to communicates its requirements to the BSC. The BSC uses the information to reserve and schedule its resources accordingly.

To support *rate-based* sessions, the BSC must be able to foresee how byte segments are accessed. However, one does not want the BSC to be burdened with the detailed timing of data sample delivery. The *sliding window* model enables the BSC to predict future accesses. With this model, the BSC is able to make decisions on how and when to perform read-ahead or write-behind actions. Data accesses within a session are done via the byte segment interface. A separate interface is provided to manage sessions. The next chapter describes a prototype implementation of the concept and interface covered in this chapter.

---

[4]An example is the encoding scheme of MPEG streams. In MPEG, video frames do not have to appear in a stream in the same order as they are presented at the output device. The video frames can be re-ordered such that small size frames are interleaved with large size frames. The objective is to minimise the data rate variation of the stream. This is necessary in order to be compatible with fixed-rate storage devices, such as CD-ROMs. Buffering is the only way to absorb the data rate variations. The memory buffer is only of limited size and hence can only work with small data rate variations.

9

Rate-based Sessions: Prototype Implementation & Evaluation

In this chapter, a prototype implementation of *rate-based* sessions is described and its performance is evaluated.

The main purpose of this prototype is to establish the feasibility of *rate-based* sessions. In general, simple and direct approaches are chosen in preference to more complex ones. It is not meant to be an optimal solution but rather a demonstration of the concept. Further research can produce better approaches but this is beyond the purpose and scope of this thesis.

The design of the prototype is described in section 9.1. This is followed by an evaluation of the prototype performance.

9.1 Prototype Implementation

The prototype is built on top of the BSC design that was described in chapter 6. However, when a session is established, additional data and control structures are set up.

Figure 9.1 shows how a session is managed. A session has two asynchronous threads of control.

Presentation thread This translator thread reads or writes session data through the byte segment interface.

Background thread This BSC thread performs read-ahead or write-behind for the session.

Notice that, in figure 9.1, both the translator and the BSC are depicted as running in the same process. If they are implemented as separate processes, they have to communicate via inter-process calls. In that case, the role of the *presentation thread* is replaced by two communicating threads: one in the translator and the other in the BSC. For clarity, the single process model is assumed in the following discussion but the discussion is equally valid for the two-process case.

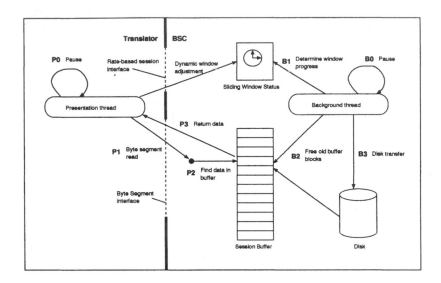

Figure 9.1: Rate-based Session Implementation. A rate-based session has two asynchronous threads of control: the presentation thread and the background thread. The sequences of actions performed by the presentation thread and the background thread are labelled as P0-P3 and B0-B3 respectively. Notice that there are two interfaces between the translator and the BSC. The byte segment interface is for data access and the rate-based session interface is for dynamic adjustment of the sliding window.

Data Accesses

Although data are accessed through the same byte segment interface as ordinary accesses externally, the BSC handles these accesses in a different way internally. Data transferred in a session are cached in a *session buffer*. A *session buffer* consists of a number of buffer blocks dedicated to store the data of a session. Data for session read accesses are read from the *session buffer*. The accesses are rejected if the requested data are not cached. Data for session write accesses are written into the *session buffer* **only** if there is space preallocated to store the data. Otherwise, the requests are rejected.

The data cached in the *session buffer* are determined by the state of the *sliding window* (section 8.4). Notice that the state of the *sliding window* is **not** verified on a per data access basis but is sampled at a much longer interval by the *background* thread.

Read-ahead/Write-behind

Periodically, the *background* thread determines the progress of the session by examining the state of the *sliding window*. If the state indicates that enough buffer space can be freed, the thread then reads more data from disk to replenish the *session buffer*. Similarly for a write session, the thread writes back data to disk when enough data are accumulated in the *session buffer*.

9.1.1   Progress Monitoring

The progress of a session is determined by the state of the *sliding window*. Internally, the BSC records the position and size of the window at a certain time. Using this information, it is straightforward to calculate the position and size of the window at any time later than the reference point. When a *background* thread is about to transfer some data for the session, it calculates the current position of the window and records the result as the new reference point.

The size and position of the window may also be changed by the adjust_window and set_window operations (section 8.5.2). To carry out these operations, the BSC calculates and records the new size and position of the window.

9.1.2   Storage Allocation

Extent-based allocation is used to allocate disk blocks to byte segments (section 6.5). The size of an extent is variable and is determined by the disk block allocator. However, it is always a multiple of the minimum extent size (section 6.4). The choice of the minimum extent size has to be balanced between higher sequential I/O throughput and the chance of finding the required number of contiguous blocks. A larger extent size means that a larger number of blocks can be transferred sequentially. However, when the disk free space is fragmented into discontiguous chunks, there is less chance of finding free space for larger extents. Also, a larger extent size means less effective space utilisation because more space is wasted in a partially filled extent. For experimentation purposes, a minimum extent size of 128 blocks (1 Kbytes block) is chosen and is the same irrespective of the data rate of the continuous-medium data. Future experience with the use of the service will provide useful feedback on choosing a suitable minimum extent size.

9.1.3   Read-ahead and Write-behind Scheduling

Essentially, the BSC performs a read-ahead action to read in a number of blocks for a session when enough blocks in the session buffer are free. Read-ahead (and the same applies to write-behind) have to be performed in time so that a session buffer always (or at a high probability) contains the valid data required by the progress of the session *sliding window*. This condition must hold at all times, including the periods when read-aheads are being performed.

To achieve this, it is necessary to estimate the service time to complete a read-ahead action. However, the actual read-ahead service time, is not constant and is dependent on a number of factors:

1. The time to complete disk transfers is obviously an important factor. This timing component is influenced by the variation in the disk seek time and rotational latency.

2. A disk transfer for a session may be delayed by other session transfers.

3. The processing of a read-ahead action may be pre-empted by other higher priority tasks, such as the processing of byte segment accesses which are more time critical.

Given a method to estimate the service time, it is possible to derive algorithms to schedule read-ahead actions for simultaneous sessions.   Indeed, research work (*e.g.* [RV91] [AOG92] [GC92] [LS93]) has been done in this area and scheduling algorithms have been derived. The research projects take into account of (1) and (2) listed above but none of them considers the effect of (3). All of them attempt to provide **hard real-time guarantees** on data delivery and the calculations involved are quite complex. It is too early to see how useful these algorithms are in practice (the results reported so far are largely based on simulations). In fact, there are two reservations about these hard real-time approaches.

Firstly, hard real-time guarantees mean that resources have to be reserved to cater for the worst-case scenario. This can lead to under utilisation of resources and unnecessary rejection of new sessions (section 8.3.3).

Secondly, it is difficult to give an accurate estimate of the service time. The actual service time can vary greatly:

- The disk seek time depends on the relative position of the disk head and the location on the disk platter where the data are stored.

- The queueing delay of a disk transfer is affected by the schedule of other sessions. When all sessions are of constant rate, this delay is calculable because disk transfers for these sessions are isochronous. When some or all sessions are variable rate, accurate estimation of the queueing delay becomes very difficult. It is not possible to know *a priori* the actual data consumption rate of these sessions. Hence it is not possible to know in advance the relative timing of the read-ahead actions of different sessions because the precise moments to schedule read-ahead actions depend on the consumption rate of sessions.

- The pre-emption of read-ahead processing by other higher priority tasks is even more difficult to estimate. On a lightly loaded system where CPU cycles is not a limiting resource, the effect of this delay on the service time may be negligible relative to the other two factors. However, when the CPU loading is high, this factor can significantly delay the read-ahead processing. Unfortunately, it is difficult to estimate this source of delay because it depends on the tasks the system happens to be doing and may be completely independent of the read-ahead activities.

Given that the service time is difficult to estimate accurately, a significant "slack" time has to be included in the estimation to cater for the variation. With this built-in "slack" time, it is not clear whether there is any more need for precise scheduling of read-ahead actions for multiple concurrent sessions, as the hard real-time approaches tend to produce. A simpler scheduling approach, such as first-come-first-serve, which relies on the built-in "slack" to absorb any service time variation may be sufficient.

Chosen solution

In the prototype, the **same** number of blocks are read in read-ahead actions, irrespective of the difference in the data rate of the sessions. All the blocks in a transfer fall within an extent. As disk blocks in an extent are contiguous, the disk transfers are strictly sequential.

A read-ahead action is performed whenever the number of free blocks in a session buffer equals the transfer size. Concurrent read-ahead actions are handled on a first-come-first-served basis. However, sufficient buffer space is allocated to sessions to cater for the case in which *all* active sessions have to be serviced simultaneously. The buffer size is calculated as follows:

Suppose the size of each transfer is K blocks and the service time of a read-ahead action is T. Also for a session S with data rate R, the sliding window size is W blocks. With N active sessions in progress, the maximum queueing delay is $N * T$. Hence the minimum buffer size for session S to cater for the worst case condition in which all sessions have to be serviced simultaneously is $K + W + N * T * R$.

Naturally, the larger the number of bytes transferred in each read-ahead, the larger is the buffer size. Therefore, it is not desirable to let this number becomes too large. In the prototype, the number is chosen to be 128 blocks.

A fixed transfer size and a straightforward read-ahead scheduling method are chosen mainly because of the simplicity of the approach. As this prototype is a demonstration of concept, a simple approach is sufficient for this purpose. Moreover, in view of the discussion above on the drawbacks of providing hard real time guarantees, I believe that a more complex approach is not really necessary for delivering continuous-medium data. However, further work will have to be done to verify this claim.

This completes the description of the prototype implementation. The prototype was tested to verify that it can support *rate-based* sessions. In the next section, its performance is evaluated in more detail.

9.2 Evaluation

9.2.1 Measured Parameters

In this section, the results of a number of experiments, designed to evaluate the performance of the prototype implementation, are reported. Since write-behind is very similar to read-ahead, only read sessions are discussed below.

The following discussion will concentrate on two aspects of the prototype performance.

1. The service time of byte segment reads. This timing is called **data access service time**.

2. The service time of read-ahead actions. This timing is called **read-ahead service time**.

Data Access Service Time

There are two reasons for measuring the data access service time.

Firstly, the timing quantifies the overhead in performing byte segment accesses.

Secondly, the distribution of the service time is a good indication of any interference on byte segment accesses by the internal actions of the BSC. Although the read-ahead actions performed by the BSC ensure that byte segment accesses in *rate-based* sessions would not be delayed by disk transfers, internal actions of the BSC may interfere with byte segment accesses in other ways. It is therefore important, as part of this evaluation, to quantify such interference and to verify that its effect is tolerable.

It was explained in the previous section that there are two asynchronous threads of controls to support a *rate-based* session. They are: the *presentation thread* which performs byte segment accesses and the *background thread* which performs read-ahead actions. As the activities of the *presentation thread* are time critical, this thread should not be delayed by other threads and should be scheduled by the kernel immediately after it becomes runnable. By comparison, the *background thread* is less time critical because the period between two read-ahead actions is much longer and any delay caused by thread scheduling can be absorbed by increasing the level of buffering. Hence, *presentation threads* are all running at a priority higher than *background threads*. In this way, the kernel, which offers pre-emptive scheduling on the target platform, would always pre-empt a running *background thread* when a *presentation thread* becomes runnable.

Nevertheless, the *presentation thread* and the *background thread* of a session still have to synchronise their accesses to the *session buffer*. Hence, the *presentation thread* can still be blocked by the *background thread* if the latter is holding exclusive access to the *session buffer* when it is pre-empted. Unfortunately, this kind of interference is unavoidable. However, the blocking duration, in practice, is negligible. This is because the *background thread* only acquires exclusive access to the *session buffer* when it is about to insert or remove some buffer blocks. This action only takes a few micro seconds to complete and is only performed once per read-ahead. Nevertheless, the blocking duration should also include the extra thread switching and scheduling overheads. These overheads increase the blocking duration to around 300 μs.

To summarise, special attention was given in the implementation to minimise the interference on the activities of the *presentation threads*. The results of the experiments will verify how successfully the degree of interference is reduced.

Read-ahead Service Time

This timing quantifies the time to complete a read-ahead action. It was noted in the previous section that an estimation of this service time is needed in order to perform read-ahead in time. Also, it was asserted that an accurate estimate of the service time is difficult to obtain because the disk transfer service time, the disk transfer queueing delay and the pre-emption of read-ahead processing by higher priority tasks can vary the timing significantly. The results of the experiments will provide evidence to substantiate this claim.

9.2.2 Experimental Setup

The target platform, on which the measurements were taken, consists of a 25MHz MC68030 processor (Motorola MVME147), 8 Mbytes of volatile memory, 4 Mbytes of non-volatile memory and a 330 Mbytes (Micropolis 1378) SCSI-1 disk.

A test program was used to simulate the translator and generate byte segment accesses. Both the BSC and the test program ran on the same machine but as two different processes. In other words, the role of the *presentation thread* as described in previous discussions is performed by two communicating threads: one in the test program and the other in the BSC. The communication between the threads is done via local MSRPC calls. The two

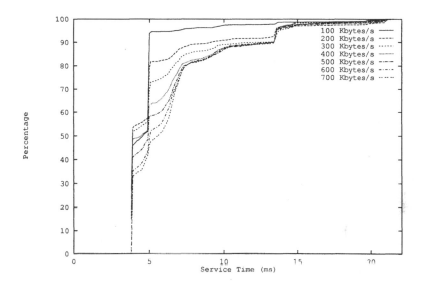

Figure 9.2: Cumulative Distribution of Single Session Data Access Service Time.

threads both run at the same priority which is higher that the priority of the *background thread*.

9.2.3   Single Session Performance

In this set of results, a single session is established in each run to read in a 10 Mbyte byte segment at a certain data rate. The data rate is constant and the size of each read request is 8Kbytes. Multiple runs were performed and each run is set to a different data rate.

Data Access Service Time

Figure 9.2 shows the cumulative frequency distribution of the data access service time for a single session at different data rates. The figure shows the service time distribution as the data rate changes from 100 Kbytes/s to 700 Kbytes/s. The prototype is capable of delivering a maximum data rate of 750 Kbytes/s. The sustained throughput of the disk, as stated in its specification, is around 1 Mbytes/s. The shortfall is likely to be caused by a combination of software and hardware overheads.

The majority of the requests are handled in less than 5 ms. This time includes a constant 2.6 ms MSRPC overhead and the time to copy 8 Kbytes from the session buffer to the IPC buffer. The sub-5ms region actually consists of two distinct bands, one at 3.9 ms and the other at 5 ms. This is just an artefact of the hardware characteristic. The 8 Mbytes main memory is made up of 4 Mbytes on the processor card and 4 Mbytes on a VME memory board. The buffer blocks that make up the *session buffer* can come from either memory banks. Unfortunately, the memory access times of the two memory banks are different.

Memory access by the processor is faster to the local memory than to the VME memory because local accesses do not have to go through the VME bus arbitration logic. It turns out that this memory access difference results in a 1 ms difference in the time spent to copy 8 Kbytes between the session buffer and the IPC buffer.

As the data rate increases, a larger percentage of the service time falls outside the 5 ms mark. This percentage rises from 5% at 100 Kbytes/s to 55% at 700 Kbytes/s. A check on the raw data reveals that the requests with the longer service time are all recorded in periods when read-ahead actions are in progress. This indicates that the activities of the *background thread* do interfere with those of the *presentation thread*.

Since the longer service time is caused by the interference by the *background thread* activities, the higher percentage of longer service time at higher data rate is expected. This is because as the data rate goes up, the *background thread* reads data from disk more often and so the chance of interference is higher.

The service time distributions above the 5 ms mark rises sharply at two points: one at the 6–7 ms mark and the other at the 13 ms mark. The two abrupt changes are separated by a large margin. This suggests that the *background thread* activities interfere with the *presentation thread* activities in two different ways.

The change at the 6–7 ms mark can be attributed to contention between the disk transfer DMA and the processor memory accesses. This is a limitation of the hardware and cannot be avoided by any software means.

The source of interference which results in the change at the 13 ms mark, is more difficult to identify. In fact, no verifiable explanation was found to account for this behaviour. The service time increase is so large that it is very unlikely to be caused by any contention at the hardware level. At the software level, the *presentation thread* could be blocked by the exclusive access held by the *background thread*. But even so the blocking duration would be far too small to account for the big increase in service time. A plausible explanation of the behaviour, in the absence of a better one, is that the kernel has not pre-empted the *background thread* immediately, as it should have done, when the *presentation thread* is ready to run. The time scope of this work does not allow for a detailed investigation into the cause of this anomaly. However, once the cause is identified in future, the problem should not be difficult to resolve.

Read-ahead Service Time

Figure 9.3 shows the distribution of the read-ahead service time under two different conditions. Figure 9.3a shows the distribution with the *presentation thread* deliberately changed to perform no read access. Hence, the variation in service time comes purely from the disk transfer time. Figure 9.3b shows the distribution under the normal condition in which the *presentation thread* performs read accesses concurrently.

As expected, the service time distribution without any presentation activity (figure 9.3a) is independent of the data rate. The disk block allocator allocates blocks for the whole byte segment contiguously[1]. Therefore, the disk transfers are strictly sequential.

The 10 percentile and the 90 percentile of the service time distribution are 136 ms and 153 ms respectively. This variation can be accounted for by the rotational latency (16.67ms

---

[1]The allocator uses a first-fit algorithm and always tries to allocate contiguous blocks to byte segments as they extend.

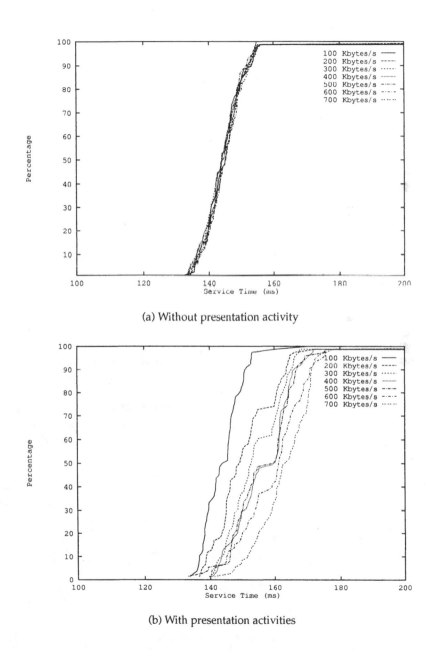

(a) Without presentation activity

(b) With presentation activities

Figure 9.3: Cumulative Distribution of Single Session Read-ahead Service Time.

maximum) and the single track seek which is necessary if a read has to continue on the next cylinder. Each cylinder holds 285 Kbytes, so for 128 Kbytes reads, every other read involves a single track seek (5 ms).

When the *presentation thread* is active (figure 9.3a), the service time increases with the data rate. At 100 Kbytes/s, the service time distribution is the same as the non-active case. At 700 Kbytes/s, the 10 percentile and the 90 percentile increase to 152 ms and 171 ms respectively. This represents an average increase of 12 % over the non-active case. Since all other factors remain the same, the increase in service time can only be caused by the interference of the read-ahead processing by the high priority *presentation thread*.

From this set of results, the service time varies between 136 ms (10 percentile at 100 Kbytes/s) and 171 ms (90 percentile at 700 Kbytes/s). Also, the variation introduced by the disk transfer time and the interference of read-ahead processing by the higher priority thread are of the same magnitude.

9.2.4 Multiple Session Performance

In this set of results, multiple sessions are established in each run and each session read in a **different** 10 Mbyte byte segment at the **same** data rate (100 Kbytes/s). Like the single session experiments, the data rate is constant and the size of each read request is 8 Kbytes. Multiple runs were performed and each run has a different number of sessions.

Data Access Service Time

Figure 9.4 shows the cumulative frequency distribution of the data access service time of a session when different number of sessions are active concurrently.

At the same aggregate data rate, the service time in this case is generally worse that the single session case. The difference becomes more prominent with more concurrent sessions. However, the apparent deterioration is not because of any change in the processing time of the requests. Instead, the main difference between this and the single session case is that multiple *presentation threads* are active and these threads can pre-empt each other.

When an event occurs, such as a timeout, which causes a thread to become runnable, the kernel would perform a thread re-schedule. This action would pre-empt the running thread if other runnable thread(s), such as the thread which has just become runnable, is at the same or at a higher priority than the running thread. Therefore, a presentation thread may be pre-empted by other presentation threads which run at the same priority. This behaviour has the effect of delaying the completion of the request processing and increasing the service time of the request.

Read-ahead Service Time

Table 9.1 shows the average read-ahead service time for each session in a multi-session run. Here, the disk transfer queueing delay dominates the service time. The sessions all start at the same time, have the same data rate, perform read-ahead isochronously and are in-phase with each other. Hence, the disk transfers appear in bursts and some sessions suffer longer queueing delay than others. Also, the queueing delay is a function of the number of active sessions and the disk transfer time of the sessions.

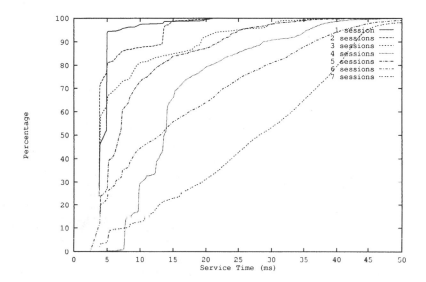

Figure 9.4: Cumulative Distribution of Multiple Session Data Access Service Time.
The data rate of each session is 100 Kbytes/s.

Average Read-ahead Service Time (ms)						
No. of	Session No.					
sessions	1	2	3	4	5	6	7
1	144	-	-	-	-	-	-
2	169	314	-	-	-	-	-
3	197	335	511	-	-	-	-
4	185	291	476	651	-	-	-
5	187	320	471	589	776	-	-
6	232	343	488	667	803	988	-
7	250	268	518	688	753	1001	1032

Table 9.1: Average Read-ahead Service Time with Multiple Sessions.

The queueing delay may be reduced by arranging the sessions to perform read-ahead actions out-of-phase so that a disk transfer for a session is not delayed by disk transfers for other sessions. Recall that the buffering requirement of sessions is directly related to the read-ahead service time because enough data must be cached in the buffer to cover the duration of a transfer, reducing the queueing delay would reduce the service time and the buffering requirement. For fixed-rate sessions, this can be done simply by adjusting the starting time of sessions to ensure that they are out-of-phase. The phase relations of the sessions will be maintained thereafter because of the isochronous nature of the sessions. On the other hand, it is not possible to fix the phase relations of variable-rate sessions because each session consumes data at a varying rate and the intervals between consecutive read-ahead actions are variable. Hence, there is no simple way to ensure that variable-rate sessions would not perform read-ahead in-phase with each other. Sufficient buffer space has to be allocated to the sessions to cater for this situation.

Apart from the disk transfer queueing delay, multiple sessions also have other effects on the read-ahead service time. These effects can be seen by looking at the service time distribution of the session in a multi-session run which does not suffer from queueing delay. Figure 9.5 shows the cumulative distribution of the read-ahead service time for this category of sessions. As in the single session case, the figure shows the distribution with (figure 9.5a) and without (figure 9.5b) presentation activity.

Without any presentation activity (figure 9.5a), the service time apparently increases with more sessions. However, there is no direct relation between the two. In fact, the disk seek time is the contributing factor to the increase. In a multi-session run, consecutive disk transfers are for different sessions. After a disk transfer for a session is completed, the disk head is at the wrong location for the next transfer and a disk seek is necessary before data for the next transfer can be read. Using the single session case (in which disk transfers are strictly sequential) as the base line, the disk seek has increased the service time by an average of 40 ms in the worst case (the 7-session run).

When the *presentation threads* are active (figure 9.5b), the service time again increases with the number of sessions. This increase can be attributed to the interference of the read-ahead processing by the activities of the higher priority *presentation threads*.

From this set of results, the service time varies between 136 ms (10 percentile in the 1-session run) and 235 ms (90 percentile in the 7-session run). In other words, the service time can be 73% larger than the minimum value.

It was asserted earlier that the read-ahead service time can vary significantly. The above experiments have provided the empirical evidence to substantiate this claim.

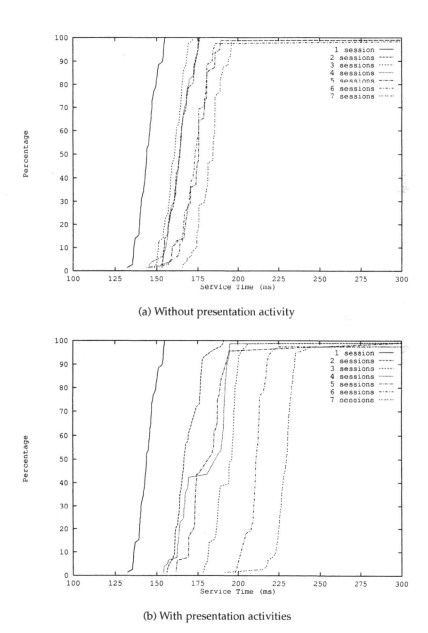

(a) Without presentation activity

(b) With presentation activities

Figure 9.5: Cumulative Distribution of Multiple Session Read-ahead Service Time.
The data rate of each session is 100 Kbytes/s.

10

Conclusion

This dissertation presented a network storage architecture that supports multiple file abstractions and is readily extensible. This chapter summarises the main conclusions, and suggests possible further work.

10.1 Summary

Most contemporary distributed file systems are not designed to be extensible. This work asserts that the lack of extensibility is a problem (chapter 2) because:

- New data types, such as continuous-medium data and structured data, are significantly different from conventional unstructured data, such as text and binary, that contemporary distributed file systems are built to support.

- Value-adding clients can provide functional enhancements, such as convenient and reliable persistent programming and automatic and transparent file indexing, but cannot be integrated smoothly with contemporary distributed file systems.

- New media technologies, such as the optical jukebox and RAID disk, can extend the scale and performance of a storage service but contemporary distributed file systems do not have a clear framework to incorporate these new technologies and to provide the necessary user level transparency.

Motivated by these observations, the new network storage architecture (MSSA) presented in this dissertation, is designed to be extensible. Design modularity is taken as the key to achieve service extensibility. Common functionalities are factored into layers. Each layer adds value to the services provided by the set of lower layers.

The architectural framework (chapter 3) takes into account the need to support multiple file classes and to make all storage resources accessible to all file classes. A two layer internal structure is chosen. The physical storage layer is responsible for the management of data on secondary storage. It exports a single abstraction— the byte segment— to the

117

logical storage layer. The logical storage layer provides different file classes, such as the flat file, structured file and continuous-medium file; and uses byte segments to store file data.

It is anticipated that different media technologies and different storage organisation strategies will be used. Furthermore, the service should be readily extensible with new file classes. For these reasons, the object-container model is adopted. Objects, i.e. byte segments or files, are collected in containers. Different byte segment implementations are distinguished by different byte segment containers. Different file classes are segregated into different file containers. New file classes and new byte segment implementations can be added with new containers and do not affect existing ones. Also, a file container may be mapped to a number of byte segment containers, each of which encapsulates a different byte segment implementation.

The main characteristic of the architecture is the building of services in multiple layers. In order to establish the feasibility of this multi-layer approach, this work examines a number of key design issues and concentrates on how the interactions between layers can be accommodated.

- This work recognises that a flexible access control mechanism is necessary for a multi-layer architecture (chapter 4). Value-adding clients should be able to transfer access rights to end-clients temporarily to shorten the data access paths. Similarly, the interactions between end-clients and network services can be simplified if access rights can be transferred from an end-client to a network service while the latter is performing a service for the former. For this purpose, temporary capabilities are used for access checking. However, capabilities are complemented by access control lists because the latter provides a more rigid form of control.

- This work considers how stored objects are named and located (chapter 5). Identifiers, rather than textual names, are used to avoid prejudicing the naming scheme of upper layers. Also, identifiers are more suitable for embedding in composite objects. The formats of container and object identifiers are designed to minimise the cost of resolving names in multiple layers.

- The design of a byte segment custode is presented (chapter 6). This design uses non-volatile memory to provide atomic update semantics at high performance. Atomic update semantics are desirable as, externally, there are fewer exception conditions to consider. This advantage is important because the implementation of file classes can be greatly simplified.

- Different file classes may have different performance requirements on byte segment accesses. In particular, continuous-medium data, unlike other data types, have stringent temporal requirements which must be met to ensure acceptable presentation qualities. To allow the logical storage layer to specify performance requirements on byte segment accesses, the idea of BSC sessions is introduced into the architecture. This idea is applied to continuous-medium data delivery. The semantics and the use of this kind of session (*rate-based*) are presented (chapter 8).

A prototype implementation of the byte segment custode is operational. Performance measurements obtained from the prototype (chapter 7) confirm that atomic update semantics can be provided at high performance. The idea of *rate-based* sessions is also tested with a prototype implementation (chapter 9). Its performance was measured (chapter 9). The results verify the feasibility of the idea.

To conclude, this work has proposed a clear framework to construct an extensible network storage service. As many design aspects were considered as time and resource allowed. Key concepts, such as *rate-based* sessions and the use of non-volatile memory to support atomic byte segment updates, have been prototyped. Other components of the design can be drawn from related work in the Computer Laboratory (such as HLSS) or are well understood (such as the flat file custode). I expect the design will evolve as more experience with it is gained but the underlying principle, i.e. the emphasis on design modularity to achieve service extensibility, will stand.

10.2 Further Work

Currently, the BSC only supports single update atomicity. The basic NVRAM transaction facility can be further exploited by extending the design to group together multiple updates to a byte segment into a single atomic transaction. Externally, these transactions can be identified by BSC sessions. Atomic transactions are usually considered as too costly to be used in network storage services. Using non-volatile memory, the BSC prototype has shown that performance need not be sacrificed to support atomic semantics. Further research is needed to fully exploit the potential of this improved semantics.

The implementation of *rate-based* sessions is a prototype. Although the measurements taken under artificial loads are encouraging, experience with actual use is needed to identify better policies to perform resource reservation and scheduling. Also, experience with real workloads will help to determine whether statistical multiplexing of variable rate streams will allow bandwidth gain or whether peak rate allocation is unavoidable.

The CFC and different translators for different encoding formats have to be implemented. Another issue which deserves further investigation is whether resource reservation should be extended to cover multiple streams presented in sequence. Multi-media documents may consist of multiple video/audio clips that must be presented in sequence and are sensitive to excessive delay between clips. Reserving resources for multiple streams may be necessary to ensure the smooth presentation of these documents.

This work has identified the need to support multiple storage device types and storage organisation strategies. The architectural framework is defined to separate these physical storage functions from the logical storage functions of providing different file abstractions. However, algorithms have to be developed to decide where, among the available storage options, to store file data and when to migrate file data within the physical storage layer. File access histories collected at the logical storage layer could be useful input to these algorithms.

Experience with the use of the service would help to identify where the design could be improved. Current work in the Computer Laboratory includes an investigation into a platform to support multi-media presentation. It is intended that MSSA will store the multi-media documents that are accessed by the presentation platform. Also, the extension of the storage service with value-adding clients to provide enhanced functionalities, such as replication and disconnected operation, is being investigated.

Bibliography

[AOG92]   David P. Anderson, Yoshitomo Osawa, and Ramesh Govindan. A file system for continuous media. *ACM Transactions on Computer Systems*, 10(4):311–337, November 1992.
(cited on pages 89, 106)

[ASTvR86]   S. J. Mullender A. S. Tanenbaum and R. van Renesse. Using sparse capabilities in a distributed operating system. In *Proceeding of the 6th International Conference on Distributed Computing Systems*, pages 558–563. IEEE, May 1986.
(cited on page 38)

[Bac86]   Maurice J. Bach. *The Design of the UNIX Operating System*. Prentice-Hall International, 1986. ISBN 0-13-201757-1 025.
(cited on page 6)

[BAD⁺92]   Mary Baker, Satoshi Asami, Etienne Deprit, John Ousterhout, and Margo Seltzer. Non-volatile memory for fast, reliable file systems. In *Proceedings of the fifth International Conference on Architectural Support for Programming Languages and Operating Systems*, pages 10–22, October 1992.
(cited on pages 86, 87)

[BBLP86]   Jean-Pierre Banâtre, Michel Banâtre, Guy Lapalme, and Florimond Ployette. The design and building of enchere, a distributed electronic marketing system. *Communications of the ACM*, 29(1):19–29, January 1986.
(cited on page 67)

[BFH⁺67]   D. W. Barron, A. G. Fraser, D. F. Hartley, B. Landy, and R. M. Needham. File handling at cambridge university. In *Proceedings of AFIPS Spring Joint Computer Conference*, pages 163–167. The American Federation of Information Processing Societies, May 1967.
(cited on page 41)

[Bhu71] A K Bhushan. File Transfer Protocol. Request for comments 114, National Information Center, April 1971. Not online. Updated by RFC 141, RFC 172, RFC 171.
(cited on page 5)

[BKT85] Mark Brown, Karen Kolling, and Edward Taft. The Alpine File System. *ACM Transactions on Computer Systems*, 3(4):261–293, November 1985.
(cited on pages 6, 60)

[BMTW91] Jean Bacon, Ken Moody, Sue Thomson, and Tim Wilson. A multi-service storage architecture. *ACM Operating Systems Review*, 25(4):47–65, October 1991.
(cited on page 56)

[BRAC91] A. Lester Buck and Jr. Robert A. Coyne. Dynamic hierarchies and optimization in distributed storage systems. In *The 11th IEEE Mass Storage Symposium*, pages 85–91, 1991.
(cited on page 14)

[Bur88] Michael Burrows. Efficient data sharing. Technical Report 153, University of Cambridge Computer Laboratory, December 1988. The author's PhD thesis.
(cited on pages 6, 7)

[CAK+92] Sailesh Chutani, Owen T. Anderson, Michael L. Kazar, Bruce W. Leverett, W. Anothony Mason, and Robert N. Sidebotham. The episode file system. In *Proceedings of USENIX Winter Conference*, pages 43–60. USENIX, January 1992.
(cited on pages 60, 86)

[Cal87] R. S. Calnan. Island: A distributed multimedia system. In *Proceedings of IEEE Globecom'87*, pages 744–748, Tokyo, November 1987.
(cited on pages 6, 89, 91)

[CH91] Greg Cockroft and Leo Howritz. Nextstep: Putting JPEG to multiple users. *Communications of the ACM*, 34(4):45, April 1991.
(cited on page 9)

[CKKS89] George Copeland, Tom Keller, Ravi Krishnamurthy, and Marc Smith. The case for safe ram. In *Proceedings of the Fifteenth International Conference on Very Large Data Bases*, 1989.
(cited on page 61)

[CMR+90] A. Chang, M. F. Mergen, R. K. Rader, J. A. Roberts, and S. L. Porter. Evolution of storage facilities in AIX version 3 for RISC System/6000 processors. *IBM Journal of Research and Development*, 34(1):103–105, January 1990.
(cited on pages 60, 86)

[Cra86] Stephen Christopher Crawley. The Entity system: An object-based filing system. Technical Report 86, University of Cambridge, April 1986. The author's Phd thesis.
(cited on page 6)

[CS92] Scott Carson and Sanjeev Setia. Optimal write batch size in log-structured file systems. In *Proceedings of USENIX File Systems Workshop*, pages 79–91. USENIX, May 1992.
(cited on page 84)

[Del80] Carl Dellar. Removing backing store administration from the CAP operating system. *ACM Operating Systems Review*, 14(4):41–49, October 1980.
(cited on page 6)

[DH66] J. B. Dennis and E. C. Van Horn. Programming semantics for multipro-grammed computations. *Comunications of the ACM*, 9(3):143–155, March 1966.
(cited on page 37)

[Dio80] Jeremy Dion. The Cambridge File Server. *ACM Operating Systems Review*, 14(4):26–35, October 1980.
(cited on pages 6, 38, 49, 60)

[Dix91] Micheal Joseph Dixon. System support for multi-service traffic Technical Report 245, Computer Laboratory, University of Cambridge, September 1991. The author's Phd thesis.
(cited on page 76)

[EGLT76] K.P. Eswaran, J.N. Gray, R.A. Lorie, and I.L. Traiger. The notions of consis-tency and predicate locks in a database system. *Communications of the ACM*, 19(11):624–633, November 1976.
(cited on page 62)

[ES92] Robert M. English and Alexander A. Stepanov. Loge: a self-organizing disk controller. In *Proceedings of USENIX Winter Conference*, pages 237–241. USENIX, January 1992.
(cited on page 85)

[FO81] Marek Fridrich and W. Older. The FELIX File Server. In *The Eighth Symposium on Operating Systems Principles*, pages 37–44. ACM, December 1981.
(cited on pages 6, 60)

[fta85] Open   Systems   Interconnection: File   transfer, access and management iso/dis/8571. British Standards Institution DD113, 1985.
(cited on page 5)

[Gal91] Didier Le Gall. MPEG: A video compression standard for multimedia appli-cations. *Communications of the ACM*, 34(4):46–58, April 1991.
(cited on page 9)

[GC92] J. Gemmell and S. Christodoulakis. Principles of delay-sensitive multimedia data storage and retrieval. *ACM Transaction on Information System*, 10(1):51–90, January 1992.
(cited on pages 89, 106)

[Gel89]   J. P. Gelb. System-managed storage. *IBM Systems Journal*, 28(1):77–103, January 1989.
(cited on page 14)

[GJSJ91] David K. Gifford, Pierre Jouvelot, Mark A. Sheldon, and James W. O'Toole Jr. Semantic file systems. In *Proceedings of 13th ACM Symposium on Operating Systems Principles*, pages 16–25. Association for Computing Machinery SIGOPS, October 1991.
(cited on page 11)

[Gon89]   Li Gong. A secure identity-based capability system. In *Proceeding of the 1989 Symposium on Security and Privacy*, pages 56–63. IEEE, May 1989.
(cited on pages 38, 45)

[Gra79]   J.N. Gray. Notes on database operating systems. In *Operating Systems: An Advanced Course*, volume 80 of *Lecture Notes in Computer Science*, pages 393–481. Springer-Verlag, 1979.
(cited on pages 60, 62)

[Hag87]   Robert Hagmann. Reimplementing the Cedar file system using logging and group commit. In *Proceedings of the 11th ACM Symposium on Operating Systems Principles*, pages 155–162, Austin TX (USA), November 1987. ACM.
(cited on pages 60, 86)

[HBM⁺89] Andy Hisgen, Andrew Birrell, Timothy Mann, Michael Schroeder, and Garret Swart. Availability and Consistency Tradeoffs in the Echo Distributed File System. In *The 2nd Workshop of Workstation Operating Systems*, pages 49–54, Pacific Grove, CA, September 1989. IEEE.
(cited on page 6)

[HCHJ91] Chris Horn, Brian Coghan, Neville Harris, and Jeremy Jones. Stable memory - another look. In A. Karshmer and J. Nehmer, editors, *International Workshop on Operating Systems of the 90s and Beyond*, number 563 in Lecture Notes in Computer Science. Springer-Verlag, 1991.
(cited on page 67)

[HKM⁺88] John H. Howard, Michael L. Kazar, Sherri G. Menees, David A. Nichols, M. Satyanarayanan, Robert N. Sidebotham, and Michael J. West. Scale and performance in a distributed file system. *ACM Transactions on Computer Systems*, 6(1):51–81, February 1988.
(cited on pages 6, 7)

[Hop90]   Andy Hopper. An experimental system for multimedia applications. *ACM Operating Systems Review*, 24(2), April 1990.
(cited on page 89)

[Inc89]   Philips International Inc. *Compact Disc- Interactive*. McGraw-Hill Book Company, 1989.
(cited on page 9)

[Jar92] Paul W. Jardetzky. Network file server design for continuous media. Technical Report 268, Computer Laboratory, University of Cambridge, October 1992. The author's PhD thesis.
(cited on pages 89, 92)

[JW91] David M. Jacobson and John Wikes. Disk scheduling algorithms based on rotational position. Technical Report HPL-CSP-91-7, Hewlett-Packard Laboratories, February 1991.
(cited on page 85)

[KH92] Gerry Kane and Joe Heinrich. *MIPS Risc architecture*. Prentice-Hall, Inc, 1992. ISBN 0-13-590472-2.
(cited on page 67)

[KLA⁺91] Michael L Kazar, Bruce W Leverett, Owen T Anderson, Vasilis Apostolides, Beth A Bottos, Sailesh Chutani, Craig F Everhart, W Anthony Mason, Shu-Tsui Tu, and Edward R Zayas. DEcorum file system architectural overview. In *Summer 1991 USENIX Conference*. USENIX Association, 1991
(cited on page 7)

[Knu73] Donald E. Knuth. *The Art of Computer Programming*, volume 1. Addison-Wesley, 2 edition, 1973.
(cited on page 76)

[KS91] James J. Kistler and M. Satyanarayanan. Disconnected operation in the Coda file system. In *Proceedings of 13th ACM Symposium on Operating Systems Principles*, pages 213–25. Association for Computing Machinery SIGOPS, October 1991.
(cited on page 6)

[Lam74] B. W. Lampson. Protection. *ACM Operating Systems Review*, 8(1), January 1974.
(cited on page 37)

[LGG⁺91] Barbara Liskov, Sanjay Ghemawat, Robert Gruber, Paul Johnson, Liuba Shrira, and Michael Williams. Replication in the Harp file system. In *Proceedings of 13th ACM Symposium on Operating Systems Principles*, pages 226–38. Association for Computing Machinery SIGOPS, October 1991.
(cited on page 6)

[LH91] Michael Liebhold and Eric M. Hoffert. Toward an open environment for digital video. *Communications of the ACM*, 34(4):103–112, April 1991.
(cited on page 9)

[Lio91] Ming Lion. Overview of the px64 kbits/s video coding standard. *Communications of the ACM*, 34(4):60–63, April 1991.
(cited on page 9)

[LS90] Eliezer Levy and Abraham Silberschatz. Distributed file systems: Concepts and examples. *Computing Surveys*, 22(4):321–374, December 1990.
(cited on pages 6, 13)

[LS93] P. Lougher and D. Shepherd. The design of a storage server for continuous media. *The Computer Journal*, 36(1):32–42, January 1993.
(cited on pages 89, 106)

[Lut91] Arch C. Luther. *Digital Video In the PC Environment*. McGraw-Hill Book Company, 1991. ISBN 0-07-039177-7.
(cited on page 9)

[MA69] S. E. Madnick and J. W. Alsop. A modular approach to file system design. In *Proceedings of AFIPS Spring Joint Computer Conference*, pages 184–189. The American Federation of Information Processing Societies, May 1969.
(cited on page 31)

[McA90] D R McAuley. Protocol design for high speed networks. Technical Report 186, Computer Laboratory, University of Cambridge, January 1990. The author's Phd thesis.
(cited on page 77)

[MH88] J. Menon and M. Hartung. The IBM 3990 disk cache. In *Proceedings of COMP-CON 1988*, pages 146–151, June 1988.
(cited on pages 61, 86)

[Mil90] D. L. Mills. On the accuracy and stablity of clocks synchronised by the network time protocol in the internet system. *ACM Computer Communication Review*, 20(1):65–75, January 1990.
(cited on page 42)

[MJLF84] Marshall K. Mckusick, William N. Joy, Samuel J. Leffler, and Robert S. Fabry. A fast file system for UNIX. *ACM Transactions on Computer Systems*, 2(3):181–197, August 1984.
(cited on pages 6, 7, 86)

[MSC⁺90] J. Moran, R. Sandberg, D. Coleman, J. Kepecs, and B. Lyon. Breaking through the nfs performance barrier. In *Proceedings of EUUG Spring 1990*, pages 199–206, April 1990.
(cited on pages 61, 86)

[Nee93] Roger M. Needham. *An Advanced Course in Distributed Computing*, chapter 12. Addison-Wesley Publishing Co., 2nd edition, 1993. Sape Mullender, Editor.
(cited on page 52)

[NHM86] R M Needham, A J Herbert, and J G Mitchell. How to connect stable storage to a computer. *Operating Systems Review*, 17(1):16, November 1986.
(cited on page 67)

[NS78] R. M. Needham and M. D. Schroeder. Using encryption for authentication in large networks of computers. *Communications of the ACM*, 21(12):993–999, December 1978.
(cited on page 38)

[NWO88] M. N. Nelson, B. B. Welch, and J. K. Ousterhout. Caching in the sprite network file system. *ACM Transactions on Computer Systems*, 6(1), February 1988. *(cited on pages 6, 7)*

[POS90] Portable operating system interface (POSIX)- part i: System application programming interface (API). IEEE Std. 1003.1-1990 Standard for Information Technology, 1990. *(cited on page 6)*

[PPTT90] Rob Pike, Dave Presotto, Ken Thompson, and Howard Trickey. Plan 9 from bell labs. In *Proceedings of the summer 1990 UKUUG Conference*, pages 1–9, July 1990. *(cited on page 49)*

[RN83] M F Richardson and R M Needham. The TRIPOS Filing Machine, a front end to a file server. *ACM Operating Systems Review*, 17(5):120–128, 1983. *(cited on page 6)*

[RO91] Mendel Rosenblum and John K. Ousterhout. The design and implementation of a log-structured file system. In *Proceedings of 13th ACM Symposium on Operating Systems Principles*, pages 1–15, October 1991. *(cited on pages 7, 60, 87)*

[RV91] P. Venkat Rangan and Harrick M. Vin. Designing file systems for digital video and audio. *ACM Operating Systems Review*, 25(5):81–94, October 1991. *(cited on pages 89, 106)*

[RW93] Chris Ruemmler and John Wilkes. Unix disk access patterns. In *USENIX Winter 1993 Conference Proceedings*, January 1993. *(cited on pages 84, 86, 87)*

[Sal73] J. H. Saltzer. *Operating Systems— an Advanced Course*. Springer Verlag, 1973. On the Naming and Binding of Objects. *(cited on page 56)*

[Sal91] Jerome H. Saltzer. File system indexing, and backup. In A. Karshmer and J. Nehmer, editors, *International Workshop on Operating Systems of the 90s and Beyond*, number 563 in Lecture Notes in Computer Science, pages 13–19. Springer-Verlag, 1991. *(cited on page 11)*

[Sat91] M. Satyanarayanan. An agenda for research in large-scale distributed data repositories. In A. Karshmer and J. Nehmer, editors, *International Workshop on Operating Systems of the 90s and Beyond*, number 563 in Lecture Notes in Computer Science, pages 2–12. Springer-Verlag, 1991. *(cited on page 11)*

[SBM89] Alex Siegel, Kenneth Birman, and Keith Marzullo. Deceit: A flexible distributed file system. Technical Report TR 89-1042, Dept. of Computer Science, Cornell University, Ithaca, NY (USA), November 1989. *(cited on page 6)*

[SGK+85] Russel Sandberg, David Goldberg, Steve Kleiman, Dan Walsh, and Bob Lyon. Design and implementation of the Sun Network Filesystem. In *Proc. Summer 1985 USENIX Conf.*, pages 119–130, Portland OR (USA), June 1985. USENIX. *(cited on page 86)*

[SGN85] Michael D. Schroeder, David K. Gifford, and Roger M. Needham. A caching file system for a programmer's workstation. In *Proceedings of the 10th ACM Symposium on Operating Systems Principles*, pages 25–34, December 1985. *(cited on page 6)*

[SHN+85] M. Satyanarayanan, John H. Howard, David A. Nicols, Robert N. Sidebotham, Alfred Z. Spector, and Michael J. West. The ITC distributed file system: Principles and design. In *Proceedings of the 10th ACM Symposium on Operating Systems Principles*, pages 35–50. ACM, December 1985. *(cited on page 41)*

[Sit92] Richard Sites, editor. *Alpha architecture reference manual*. Digital Press, Burlington MA, 1992. *(cited on page 67)*

[SKK+90] M. Satyanarayanan, James J. Kistler, P. Kumar, M. E. Okasaki, and D. C. Steere E.H. Siegel. Coda: A highly available file system for a distributed workstation environment. *IEEE Transactions on Computers*, 39(4), April 1990. *(cited on page 6)*

[SMI80] Howard Sturgis, James Mitchell, and J. Israel. Issues in the Design and Use of a Distributed File System. *Operating Systems Review*, 14(3):55–69, July 1980. *(cited on pages 6, 60)*

[SNS88] J. G. Steiner, C. Neuman, and J. I. Schiller. Kerberos: An authentication service for open network systems. In *Proceedings of the USENIX Winter Conference*, pages 191–202, February 1988. *(cited on page 38)*

[Sre92] Cormac J. Sreenan. Synchronisation services for digitial continuous media. Technical Report 292, Computer Laboratory, University of Cambridge, October 1992. The author's PhD thesis. *(cited on page 92)*

[SS75] J. H. Saltzer and M. D. Schroeder. The protection of information in computer systems. *Proceedings of the IEEE*, 63(9):1278–1308, September 1975. *(cited on page 35)*

[Sun89] Sun Microsystems, Inc. NFS: Network file system protocol specification. RFC 1094, Network Information Center, SRI International, March 1989. *(cited on pages 6, 86)*

[Svo81] Liba Svobodova. A Reliable Object-Oriented Data Repository for a Distributed Computer System. In *The Eighth Symposium on Operating Systems Principles*, pages 47–58. ACM, December 1981. *(cited on page 6)*

[Svo84]   Liba Svobodova. File servers for network-based distributed systems. *Computing Surveys*, 16(4):353–398, December 1984.
(cited on page 6)

[Tho90]   Susan E. Thomson. *A Storage Service For Structured Data*. PhD thesis, Computer Laboratory, University of Cambridge, November 1990.
(cited on pages 10, 12, 31)

[TS87]   D. B. Terry and D. C. Swinehart. Managing stored voice in the etherphone system. *ACM Operating Systems Review*, 21(5):48–61, November 1987.
(cited on pages 9, 89)

[vRST88]   Robert van Renesse, Hans Van Straveren, and Andrew S. Tanenbaum. Performance of the world's fastest distributed operating system. *Operating Systems Review*, 22(4):25–34, October 1988.
(cited on page 7)

[vRTW89]   R. van Renesse, A. S. Tanenbaum, and A. Wilschut. The design of a high-performance file server. In *Proceedings of the 9th Int. Conf. on Distributed Computing Systems*, pages 22–27. IEEE, June 1989.
(cited on page 7)

[Wal91]   Gregory K. Wallace. The JPEG still picture compression standard. *Communications of the ACM*, 34(4):31–44, April 1991.
(cited on page 9)

[Wil89]   John Wilkes. DataMesh– scope and objective, a commentary. Technical Report HPL-DSD-89-44, Hewlett-Packard Laboratories, July 1989.
(cited on page 32)

[Wil92a]   John Wilkes. DataMesh research project, phase 1. In *Proceedings of the USENIX File System Workshop*, pages 63–70, May 1992.
(cited on page 32)

[Wil92b]   Tim D. Wilson. *Increasing the performance of storage services for local area networks*. PhD thesis, Computer Laboratory, University of Cambridge, February 1992.
(cited on pages 32, 67, 87)

[WPE+83]   Bruce Walker, Gerald Popek, Robert English, Charles Kline, and Greg Thiel. The LOCUS Distributed Operating System. In *Proceedings of the Ninth ACM Symposium on Operating Systems Principles*, pages 49–70. ACM, October 1983.
(cited on page 6)

[WS91]   John Wilkes and Raymie State. Specifying data availability in multi-device file systems. *ACM Operating System Review*, 25(1):56–59, January 1991.
(cited on page 14)

[ZMB93] Wu Zhixue, Ken Moody, and Jean Bacon. A persistent programming language for multimedia databases. Technical Report TR 296, Computer Laboratory, 1993.
(cited on page 12)

Index